Dec. '83.

For Jack —

To aid your ability
to communicate to the
masses .

With Love,

Susan

Lite
English

Other books by Rudolf Flesch

Lite
English
Popular
Words
That Are
OK to Use

No Matter What William Safire, John Simon, Edwin Newman and the Other Purists Say!

by RUDOLF FLESCH

Crown Publishers, Inc. New York

Published by Crown Publishers, Inc., One Park Avenue, New York, New York 10016, and simultaneously in Canada by General Publishing Company Limited.

Manufactured in the United States of America

Library of Congress Cataloging in Publication Data

Flesch, Rudolf Franz, 1911–
  Lite English.

    1. English language—Usage—Dictionaries.
2. English language—Slang—Dictionaries. I. Title.
PE1460.F574 1983   427   83-7793
ISBN 0-517-55139-X

10 9 8 7 6 5 4 3 2 1

First Edition

*To my sister
Annie Graf*

Acknowledgment

The spelling *lite* in the title of this book follows the model of beer cans and other product labels. It is not listed in any dictionary.

There is no legal obstacle to this kind of borrowing. I simply want to acknowledge where I got the idea.

Preface

Hopefully, this book will teach you to write like a pro.

It will show you that words like *hopefully* and *pro* are now accepted. It will teach you that traditional "correct English" is now out, and slang, colloquialisms, puns and wordplays are in. It will make you sound like a live human being when you put words on paper.

To convince you that you'll be safe in following my advice I checked the usage of our most respected newspapers, magazines and journals of opinion. I looked for examples of slang and informal language in the *New York Times,* the *Wall Street Journal, Time, Newsweek, The New Yorker,* the *New Republic,* the *Nation* and the *New York Review of Books.*

The results of this one-man research project amazed me. Our most reputable, most carefully edited newspapers and magazines are full of slang and informal language. There wasn't a single issue of any of the publications I checked that didn't contain some items for my collection. "Formal English"—totally free of *any* informality—is almost a matter of the past.

What's more, there seems to be a premium on the use of slang and informal language. The highest-paid and most influential writers—columnists, critics and editorial writers—use the most relaxed and informal style. They're the most widely read journalists and know they owe it to their readers to entertain them—even when they write about politics, foreign affairs, law, taxation and other serious matters.

I used the following basic sources in writing this book: the *Oxford English Dictionary* with its three-volume *Supplement*; the unabridged *Webster's Third New International Dictionary* (cited here as *Webster's Third*); the unabridged *Random House Dictionary*; the four major current desk dictionaries— *Webster's Ninth New Collegiate Dictionary* (cited here as *Webster's Collegiate*), *Random House College Dictionary, Webster's New World Dictionary* and *American Heritage Dictionary;* the *Dictionary of American Slang* by Harold Wentworth and Stuart Berg Flexner (2d ed. 1975); and the *Barnhart Dictionary of New English Since 1963* and the *Second Barnhart Dictionary of New English.* I also used many other books on style and usage and many other dictionaries.

Everything you'll find in this book is backed by linguistic science. Don't be afraid to follow my advice in your business letters, reports, term papers and other writing jobs. Your readers will be grateful.

RUDOLF FLESCH
Dobbs Ferry, New York
March 1983

Lite
English

ad.   Since this is an alphabetically arranged book, its obvious opening is a piece on the word *ad.*

You probably think, as I did, that the word *ad* is fairly recent, but that's wrong. The first quote in the *Supplement to the Oxford English Dictionary* dates back to Thackeray, who used the word in 1841. There's also a quote from William Dean Howells, who wrote in 1902, *"Ad* is a loathly little word but we must come to it. It's as legitimate as *lunch."*

Lunch goes back to 1829. When the *Oxford English Dictionary* got around to it in 1901, the editors defined it as "a more colloquial synonym of *luncheon.* (Now the usual word exc. in specially formal use, though many persons still object to it as vulgar.)"

And so it goes. Every shortened word starts in the face of violent opposition by the stubborn adherents of "good English" and goes on to universal acceptance. *Hippo* goes back to 1872, *rhino* to 1884, *lab* to 1885. Today we have *limo* and *deli.*

So, whenever you're tempted to use the long word *advertisement,* relax and write *ad.* I found it recently (12/22/82) in a column by Russell Baker in the *New York Times.* Writing about current prices, he said, "A sculpted silverplate place setting from Italy . . . was one of the few products I found advertised in *The New Yorker* with its price listed in the ad. . . . If you wanted eight . . . it would cost you $1,290.33."

aggravate.   There are two schools of thought on the subject of English usage.

A small, ever-diminishing band of purists insists that the rules of usage have been handed down from on high and must never be broken.

The rest of us know that the English language is flexible,

settled only until further notice. Whenever the "correct" word or expression doesn't seem to fit, we adjust, change, improvise. We coin words like *humongous,* we adopt words like *chutzpah,* we say things like "Hopefully it won't rain" or "Everyone learned their lesson." Usage is king.

Take *aggravate,* for instance. *The Elements of Style* by William Strunk Jr. and E. B. White (3d ed. 1979), the current bible of the purists, says simply: *"Aggravate. Irritate.* The first means 'to add to' an already troublesome or vexing matter or condition. The second means 'to vex' or 'to annoy' or 'to chafe.'" Period.

But since 1621 people have used *aggravate* to mean "to annoy." For example (*New Republic,* 6/23/82), "Richard Nixon . . . aggravated everyone, his friends included, once he was in the White House."

Why do we use *aggravate* this way? Because there are degrees of annoyance, and for some of them words like *vex, annoy* or *irritate* are just not strong enough. Only *aggrrravate* will do.

aha!   *New York Times* columnist Russell Baker wrote about dreams (2/20/83): "I was fleeing from an immense turtle of many colors. Aha! Wait until my psychoanalyzed friends had a crack at interpreting this one."

The English language has separate interjections for *everything. Aha!* expresses satisfaction, pleasure, triumph, surprise, as in "Aha! So that's what it was!"

But that's only the first and most obvious meaning of *aha!* It isn't what Russell Baker meant. For that we must go to the secondary meaning of *aha!* It also expresses mockery, derision, irony, as in "Aha! That's what you thought but you were wrong."

The dictionaries say it all depends on the way you say it. In writing, it's harder to bring off exactly the right shade of meaning, but it's by no means impossible. If you throw in *aha!* in just the right context, readers will catch on to your tone of voice.

I ought to add that Gestalt psychologists have a technical term called the *aha reaction,* which means a sudden flash of insight or illumination. It used to be called the *aha experience,* but now psychologists have settled on *aha reaction.*

Too bad. They've taken *aha!,* a word that springs to the lips in delight or playful mockery, and made it into a dull and academic term.

ah well. Roger Rosenblatt, the brilliant columnist of *Time* magazine, wrote in a piece on the first execution by injection (12/20/82): "It seems hard to shake off the communal savagery one senses: so difficult to view revenge as anything more virtuous than active malice. Ah well, the device is new. Perhaps we only need time."

I fell to wondering about the expression *ah well* (with no comma between *ah* and *well).* I looked it up in all dictionaries and drew a complete blank. *Ah well,* though everyone knows what it means, isn't listed anywhere.

So I did a little further research. I looked up *ah* and found that it's an exclamation expressing pain, delight, regret, disgust, surprise, appreciation, pity, complaint, dislike, joy, satisfaction, relief, contempt, triumph, admiration, sorrow, lamentation, wonder, remonstrance, exultation, aversion, mockery, opposition, objection, pleasure, entreaty, boredom, plus a large variety of other emotions. In other words, it's an all-purpose exclamation to give vent to any kind of emotion.

Next I looked up *well.* The word can be used as a noun,

verb, adjective, adverb and interjection. In the phrase *ah well* it is clearly an interjection and is used, as *Webster's Collegiate* puts it, "to indicate resumption of discourse."

So, if you put *ah* and *well* together, it means something like "This is sad (or great or tragic or whatever), but never mind, let's go on. Let's shift gears and forget about our emotions." It's a sort of verbal tranquilizer.

ain't.   On January 29, 1983, President Reagan dropped a bombshell at a meeting in Boston. He said casually that the corporate income tax should be abolished. Next day, White House reporters asked Reagan's spokesman, Larry Speakes, about it. Speakes said the subject was closed. " 'It ain't going to be looked at,' he said rather heatedly" (*New York Times,* 1/31/83).

There's no doubt that Speakes used the word *ain't.* Surely, the *Times* reporter put it down the way he said it. The reporter didn't imply that Speakes was an illiterate yokel, he simply reported what was actually said.

Is it OK to say *ain't? Webster's Ninth New Collegiate Dictionary* (1983) says, "Although disapproved by many and more common in less educated speech, *ain't* is used orally in most parts of the U.S."

That doesn't mean that *ain't* can also be used in writing without upsetting readers who have been brainwashed by their English teachers. But as you can see from my example, it is now all right to quote someone saying *ain't* without branding him or her as an uneducated person.

I predict that twenty years from now *ain't* will take its place in formal writing.

alibi.   *Alibi* is a Latin word meaning "elsewhere." In English it is a legal term. According to Giffis's *Law Dictionary* it is "a provable account of an individual's whereabouts at the time of the commission of a crime which would make it impossible or impracticable to place him at the scene of the crime."

That's clear enough, but since 1912 people have been using the word in the sense of *any* kind of excuse, much to the annoyance of purists. They've fought against this usage strenuously, but by now their fight is just about over. All dictionaries list the meaning of excuse for *alibi,* although the *Oxford American Dictionary* (1980) still adds a note, "Careful writers avoid use of *alibi* when only an excuse is intended."

This state of affairs leaves us with a puzzling question. Why is it that people are using *alibi* in the sense of excuse? On the face of it, the leap from a highly specific sense to a very broad one seems inexplicable.

I think I know the answer to this little puzzle. For almost a century people have been reading mystery stories. A prominent feature of almost all of them is the offer of an alibi, carefully concocted by the murder suspect. It's then the job of the Great Detective to break that alibi, using vast amounts of time-consuming effort and incredible ingenuity.

Readers of mystery stories—which means most of the literate population—are therefore in the habit of suspecting *any* alibi, knowing full well that in the end it will turn out to be an elaborate fake.

And so the word *alibi* came to mean a phony excuse.

Recently (11/22/82), the City Hall reporter of *The New Yorker,* Andy Logan, started an article this way: "People who consider themselves too busy to keep up with state and local political campaigns often use the excuse that most of these spectacles offer little more than predictable plots, interchangeable dialogue, and the same old central-casting political types. Some other alibi for inattention to the democratic process has to be found in the case of this year's statewide election in New York."

As you see, Andy Logan used *alibi* correctly in the current sense of phony excuse.

all that jazz.   Among the unsigned "Topics" on the editorial page of the *New York Times* (11/18/82), there was a brief article dealing with a Chinese pamphlet against American-style jazz. The headline on that item read

All That Jazz

Now we all know what jazz means, although few of us probably know—I didn't—that the word is possibly derived from the Creole word *jass,* meaning sexual intercourse. But what does *jazz* mean in the phrase "and all that jazz"?

Three of the four major desk dictionaries—*Webster's New World, Random House College,* and *American Heritage*— say the phrase is slang and means "remarks, acts, concepts, etc. regarded as hypocritical, tiresome, trite, pretentious, etc."

Obviously this type of jazz has absolutely nothing to do with the Chinese pamphlet. The headline "All That Jazz" was picked simply to dress the item up and give the reader a little extra pleasure and mild amusement.

Fifty years ago the writer of that jazzy, slangy headline might have been reprimanded and the headline corrected in a later edition to read, dully, "Chinese Pamphlet Against Jazz."

Times have changed and slang words, puns, all kinds of fun and games are now permitted or even encouraged on West 43d Street.

It's a little like an elephant learning to dance, but it sure is welcome.

ante.   *Ante* is a poker term. It's what you must put up before you get your first cards or exchange cards for new ones.

Fifty years ago, in the days of the famous play *The Front Page,* you'd expect newspapermen to play poker—with their hats on—and to use poker language in their stories. But today, among *New York Times* staff members, that seems unlikely.

Still, there came the day (11/7/82) when a piece about India described the new political demands of the Sikhs, a large religious group that lives in the Punjab, north of Delhi. They want semi-independence for the Punjab, leaving the central government only defense, foreign affairs, railroads and the currency.

The *Times* copyreader looked at this story and decided on a headline. What do you think it said? It fell back on poker:

Sikhs Raise the Ante at a Perilous Cost to India

This is something of a record. Not only is it slang, it's poker slang. And not only that, the copyreader went out of his way to use *ante* in the headline. The word did *not* appear in the article.

Slang is now used freely in *Times* headlines to give its readers some extra fun.

Good for the *Times.*

anxious.   The *Oxford American Dictionary* (1980) calls itself "the first modern paperbound dictionary to lay down the law on correct grammar." About the word *anxious,* for instance, it says: "1. troubled and uneasy in mind. 2. causing worry, filled with such feeling, *an anxious moment.* 3. eager, *anxious to please.* . . . Careful writers do not use *anxious* in its third sense. They would write *eager to please.*"

Like most other Americans, *New York Times* writers pay no attention to this arbitrary rule. In a recent article on possible

Republican successors to President Reagan, the *Times* said (12/20/82): "No one wants to appear anxious to shove the President into retirement."

Aside from diehards like the *Oxford American Dictionary*, the purists have just about lost the fight over *anxious*. Most dictionaries and usage books now accept the prevailing meaning of *eager*.

Popular language likes to exaggerate. When something is fine, we say it's terrific. When things are bad, we say they're awful. When we don't like something, we say we hate it. And when we're eager, we say we're anxious.

argle-bargle.   In the *New Republic* (2/28/83) George V. Higgins wrote about the ten-year-long court battle over the Boston public schools. "None of this argle-bargle," he wrote, "made the schools the least bit more appealing to parents of white children."

Argle-bargle sounds like recent slang, but it isn't. It goes back to at least 1827, which is the date of this charming quote in the *Oxford English Dictionary:* "Me and the minister were just argle-bargling some few words on the doctrine of the camel and eye of the needle."

The dictionaries say the word is basically Scottish. Whether the Scots are especially given to long-drawn-out wrangling they don't say. Anyway, *argle-bargle* is a nice mix of *argue* and *haggle*, doubled for good measure to show the endlessness of the process.

In 1927 the *Observer* wrote: "Can they stand up to a good and sufficient argle-bargle that lasts for the best part of three hours?"

A hassle, you see, is always unpleasant. But that's not necessarily true of an argle-bargle. For some people a good, prolonged argle-bargle is downright enjoyable.

ass.   During the election of 1982, Mrs. Florence M. Sullivan, candidate for the U.S. Senate from New York, called her opponent, Senator Daniel Patrick Moynihan, a "pompous ass." The *New York Times* (11/3/82) duly reported this, obviously considering the epithet "fit to print."

In spite of her unusual outspokenness, Mrs. Sullivan lost the election by a wide margin.

There are, as you probably know, two words spelled and pronounced "ass." One means a part of the human body and I'll not concern myself with that one here.

The other word *ass* means the animal whose picture always graces the page where the word appears in the dictionary. It's an old, old word, going back to the Latin word *asinus* and to a still more ancient language of Asia Minor. Since at least 1578 the word has been used to mean "an ignorant fellow, a perverse fool, a conceited dolt," as the *Oxford English Dictionary* neatly puts it. It adds: "Now disused in polite literature and speech."

Those words were written in the 1880s. A hundred years later, they are clearly obsolete. Aside from Mrs. Sullivan, millions of people have spoken and written of pompous asses, stupid asses, stubborn asses and other asses without benefit of adjective.

Ass, meaning a person, is neither colloquial nor informal nor slang.

If you call someone an ass, you're using Shakespearean English.

aw shucks.   Anthony Lewis, the *New York Times* columnist, wrote recently (2/20/83): "A good part of Reagan's appeal may be the way he comes on as a bewildered ordinary guy, vulnerable, blundering at times but aw shucks."

What exactly does *aw shucks* mean? *Aw* is an expression of mild disgust. But what's *shucks?*

To shuck means to shell or husk, to remove the outer covering of corn, oysters, clams, peas, nuts. The shucks are the worthless pieces you get rid of. Therefore when you say *shucks* you say, "Well, it was no good anyway."

Aw shucks is one of those ingenious English expressions that condense a whole bundle of emotions. It's the tale of the fox and the sour grapes, the mental adjustment of writing off a disappointment, the physical act of shrugging off something that can't be helped.

Aw shucks is stronger than *ah well.* It wipes the emotional slate clean. You say *aw,* which means regret. Then, in the same breath, you say *shucks.* It cancels out the *aw.*

Aw shucks means "Let's have no vain regrets."

baloney.   Anthony Lewis, the *New York Times* columnist, recently (12/2/82) called former Vice-President Mondale's protectionist rhetoric "primitive baloney."

Baloney, according to the dictionaries, means pretentious nonsense, foolishness, exaggerated talk, false information, tripe, hokum, hot air, blah. All dictionaries agree that the word is slang, and that it comes from *bologna sausage.*

That's quite clear, but one problem remains. How did bologna sausage come to stand for foolish, untrue nonsense?

The dictionaries offer no theory, not even any speculation on this minor mystery. So here's my own tentative explanation. The unabridged *Random House Dictionary* defines *bologna* as "a large seasoned sausage made of finely ground meat, usually beef and pork, that has been cooked and smoked."

So *bologna* is a mixture of meat from two different kinds of animals, finely ground, cooked and smoked, until there's no detectable trace of the original ingredients—a mishmash that may or may not contain kernels of honest-to-goodness good meat.

I'm not casting aspersions on bologna sausage, which I like to eat. But there's that unmistakable link between *bologna* and *baloney.*

If more people would call baloney "baloney," it would clear the air.

bash.   First of all, there's a *bash,* which means "a thoroughly enjoyable, lively party; a wildly good time" (*Random House*). For instance, there was a *Wall Street Journal* (12/6/82) story about two famous Chinese chefs who used to cook at state banquets in Peking. "They remember whipping up dishes at one bash with 20,000 guests and also at a banquet for Richard Nixon." Whether a wildly good time was had on those occasions, the *Wall Street Journal* didn't say.

A *bash* in the sense of a party comes from the verb *bash,* which means to beat. *Bash,* in turn, has to do with *pash, dash* and *smash.*

Bashing, the heavy beating, has often been used figuratively in the past twenty years. The *Second Barnhart Dictionary of New English* lists instances of *bureaucrat-bashing, dissident-bashing, Republican-bashing* and *union-bashing.* All those violent beatings were purely verbal—no physical violence, no blood.

Recently, the *New York Times* (10/29/82) carried a headline on its top editorial that said

Bashing Japan Isn't the Answer

The editorial dealt with speeches and letters against Japanese auto imports.

Bashes and bashings have gotten pretty tame these days.

basket case.   The phrase *basket case* came into the language during World War I. It meant a soldier who had lost both arms and both legs.

In the 1970s this tragic, shocking phrase was picked up as a slang term for someone who's a nervous wreck. It began to be used quite lightheartedly. In 1972 someone was quoted in the *Saturday Review:* "I think the great distances of this country are a deterrent to long drives. Dad's a basket case by the time he gets to Yellowstone from the East."

A few years later, *basket case* began to be used for third world countries that were in extreme financial straits. Bangladesh, Bolivia, Haiti and other countries were labeled basket cases that urgently needed help.

By now, this latest meaning is widely used. *Newsweek* (11/1/82) wrote, "Spain is not yet an economic basket case."

There was no question what was meant by that sentence. Like thousands of other readers, I read it without any sense of the human tragedy the word refers to. It didn't conjure up the picture of a quadriplegic; it just meant that Spain was a long way from being as poor as Bangladesh.

Metaphors start as sharp images. As the years go by, they get paler and paler, until finally almost nothing is left of the original strength. The handicapped veterans of World War I are only a dim memory now, long overtaken by history.

batty.   Recently (10/19/82) the *New York Times* TV critic John J. O'Connor mentioned among the characters of a new show "a completely batty millionaire with a foreign accent."

Batty is undoubtedly a slang word, so labeled in most dictionaries. The *Supplement to the Oxford English Dictionary* found it in print as early as 1903 and tells us that it comes from the colloquial expression "having bats in your belfry."

Why did O'Connor pick this slang word for the dignified pages of the *New York Times?* Because it was the best word for his purpose.

Let's see. What choices did he have? I looked up *crazy* in my favorite thesaurus, *The Synonym Finder* by J. M. Rodale. Here's what I found: "insane, mad, demented, lunatic, deranged, crazed; of unsound mind, *Lat. non compos mentis;* daft, *Inf.* daffy, *Chiefly Brit. Inf.* potty, *Inf.* dotty, *Inf.* crackpot; unbalanced, touched, *Inf.* half-baked, *Brit. Sl.* bonkers, unhinged, brainsick, *Sl.* kooky, *Sl.* meshuga; *All Sl.* balmy, dippy, batty, bats, cuckoo, buggy, bughouse, bugs, screwy, wacky, wacko, goofy, loony, squirrelly, bananas, nuts, nutty, nutty as a fruitcake."

This gave O'Connor a clear choice between formal words like *insane, deranged* or *unbalanced,* all of which sound cold and clinical, and informal or slang words like *dotty* or *batty,* which sound warm, good-natured and sympathetic.

He wasn't writing a psychiatric diagnosis but a TV column, meant to inform and amuse the readers of the *New York Times.* He was paid to do a job as a professional writer, not to avoid at all costs any word that may be disapproved by dictionarymakers or English teachers. So, in his search for the exactly fitting word, he used the word *batty.*

belly up. Congressman Dan Rostenkowski, chairman of the House Ways and Means Committee, was quoted in the *New York Times* (1/7/83): "I've got to have a [Social Security] bill through the House by the end of next March. If I don't, the system goes belly up next June."

What did he mean by *belly up?* I looked for the phrase in many dictionaries and finally tracked it down in the *Second Barnhart Dictionary of New English* (1980). It says *belly up* means "flattened out; collapsed; dead" and was first spotted in 1968. The phrase is labeled slang.

There are several quotes given by Barnhart, but no derivation. The definitions convey the picture of a person lying flat on his back, dead.

Webster's Ninth New Collegiate Dictionary (1983) says *belly up* refers to a dead fish in the water. As everyone knows, fish swim with their backs up. When they die, they turn around and come to the surface, with their white belly up.

Of course this may be wrong. You're welcome to come up with an entirely different theory. It's a game everyone can play.

big deal.   The other day (11/19/82) the *New York Times* ran a playful third editorial called "The Great Token War." It dealt with the fact that people had used 17½-cent Connecticut Turnpike tokens to get 75-cent subway rides in New York City.

The editorial imagined a dialogue between New York and Connecticut. New York said, "Please, sirs, think again," etc.

Connecticut replied, "Big deal. This is your problem, not ours," etc.

So there was the slang phrase *big deal* right on the sacred editorial page of the *New York Times.*

I note with satisfaction that on November 19, 1982, the world did *not* come to an end.

On the contrary, the *Times* showed a praiseworthy deftness in writing style, using a phrase that has been in common use since 1940 to mean "sarcastically, anything or anyone believed to be unimportant, uninteresting, or unimpressive"

(Dictionary of American Slang by Wentworth and Flexner, 2d ed. 1975).

Big deal, you say? I say it's a happy event, showing continuing growth and progress of the American language.

binge. For many centuries there was an English dialect word *binge* that meant to soak a wooden vessel. Then, around 1850, the word began to be used jokingly for a drinking bout. "A man goes to the alehouse to get a good binge," a lexicographer noted in 1854. The joke caught on and to this day dictionaries define *binge* as "a drunken spree or revel."

But times change and binges are no longer looked upon as occasions of jollity and cheer. The *New York Times* (12/9/82) wrote about a psychiatric patient: "Two friends . . . visited him at the end of a three-day drug-and-alcohol binge and told him he had to get help." A few weeks earlier (11/17/82) the paper had reported that "very low doses of the drug fenfluramin, which raises brain serotonin levels, can help curb carbohydrate binges."

Binges, once celebrated by humorists, are now clinical events, treated by doctors. I wish they would let cheerful words alone. We don't have so many in the English language; let's not spoil them.

If you want to write about a prolonged overdose of drugs, alcohol or carbohydrates, call it that. But don't call it a binge.

blahs. On February 9, 1983, the *New York Times* got the blahs.

It happened in a headline, which said:

For Winter Blahs: Party on Sunday Afternoon

What are blahs? A little research yielded the following answers.

First, there's the single *blah.* It comes in two varieties, as an adjective and as a noun. As an adjective, it means mainly "bland, unexciting, unappetizing or unappealing." For example, Ngaio Marsh wrote in a mystery story (1937): "The fascinating blah stuff of hers goes down with the nitwits."

Second, there's the noun *blah,* which means nonsense, bunk, baloney. Wolcott Gibbs wrote in *The New Yorker* (1928) of "a lot of romantic blah."

Third, there's *blah-blah,* which is defined in the unabridged *Webster's Third* as "an interjection used as a derogatory comment on meaningless chatter."

And finally, we have *the blahs.* Here *Webster's Collegiate* broke new ground. It gave the definition "a feeling of boredom, discomfort, or general dissatisfaction." Always eager to provide some bit of etymology, it added, "perhaps influenced in meaning by *blasé.*" (This seems to me rather dubious. I remember an ad for an antacid, which plugged it as a weapon against the blahs.)

The 1982 *American Heritage Dictionary* listed *blahs* with the *Webster's Collegiate* definition and added the information that the word was slang.

But that didn't deter the *Times.* The first sentence of its article read, "Of all the dismal conditions the human spirit is heir to, not one stands more in need of a party to perk it up than the mid-February blahs."

blitz.   At the beginning of World War II the Germans surprised the Allies with *Blitzkrieg* (lightning war) on Poland and

France. Soon the word *blitzkrieg* got into the English language. It means, according to *Webster's Collegiate*, "war con-
ducted with great speed and force; *specif:* a violent surprise
offensive by massed air forces and mechanized ground forces
in close coordination."

The years passed and *blitzkrieg* took its place in the English language. Being awkward to pronounce, it was shortened to *blitz.*

Not only that, it gradually lost its terrifying meaning.

On October 23, 1982, I found the following headline in the
New York Times:

Trudeau Uses TV Blitz to Spell Out Nation's Plight

I read the article. It turned out that the Canadian Prime Minister had given three fifteen-minute TV speeches during that
week.

This is a blitz?

boo-boo. A boo-boo is something done by a boob,
which means a foolish or stupid person. Considering the fact
that boo-boos are made by millions of people every single
day, it's odd that the word isn't used more often in print. The
reason, of course, is the widespread prejudice against slang.
As I'm trying to prove in this book, this prejudice is rapidly
disappearing, which is why I think that *boo-boo* has a great
future.

A boo-boo is a silly, embarrassing mistake, a blunder or, as
Wentworth and Flexner's *Dictionary of American Slang* puts
it, "a faux pas." Presidents have been known to make one
boo-boo after another at their press conferences.

In a "My Turn" column in *Newsweek* (12/20/82) a space
scientist, Jack Catran, wrote about the famous movie *E.T.* and

the widespread notion that there must be Martians or aliens or "extraterrestrials" somewhere out there in space. Catran says the idea is based on "a scientific boo-boo. The UFOlogists are simply objectifying what is primarily subjective— their own faults, interests and dreams."

I think Catran has a point. The immense mythology that has been built up for many decades has somehow convinced everybody that the existence of aliens is a proven fact. Of course it isn't. It's sheer fantasy—pleasant to read about or look at in the movies, but without the slightest scientific basis.

To call this whole thing a boo-boo is downright liberating.

booze.   I'm always astonished by the age of our slang words. *Booze,* believe it or not, goes back to the year 1300. The *Oxford English Dictionary* defines the verb as "to drink deeply, or for the sake of enjoyment or goodfellowship."

As you see, *booze* has positive connotations. Boozing is pleasant, it's fun, it enhances life. That checks with the way *booze* is now used in newspapers and magazines. Pauline Kael, writing in *The New Yorker* (12/27/82) about the movie *Arthur,* said, "As the top-hatted lush, Arthur, Dudley Moore has a mad sparkle in his eyes. There's always something bubbling inside Arthur—the booze just adds to his natural fizz."

And the *New York Times* (1/2/83), commenting on another movie, *The Verdict,* said, "Paul Newman stars as a boozy ambulance-chasing lawyer who stands to be redeemed if he wins the suit."

The hero of *The Verdict is* redeemed at the end, and the movie *Arthur* has a cheerful ending. In those and other romantic movies, alcoholism is quite benign and ultimately rewarded. There's no *Lost Weekend* type of tragedy. Alcoholism may be a dread affliction, but boozing doesn't do any harm.

And so we have the word *booze,* and dozens of others, when we speak of drinking with a smile. Clinical terms like *alcoholism* or *intoxication* come up later, when we look the consequences in the eye.

broke. On the op-ed page of the *New York Times* (11/15/82), there was an article by Professor Lester Thurow of MIT on world economics. I quote: "Growth has stopped here and around the world, protection has started everywhere, whole countries are going broke." Again, later in the article, Professor Thurow writes, "The third world is broke."

The word *broke* is labeled "informal" or "slang" in most dictionaries. Why did Professor Thurow use it deliberately in his article? Because he wanted to stress the seriousness of the situation. I looked up *broke* in all the dictionaries and found the following definitions: "Ruined financially, bankrupt, penniless, without money, lacking funds, having little or no money, without money or resources, having spent all one's money."

Every single one of these words and phrases sounds vaguely euphemistic, putting some sort of fig leaf on the desperate situation. Professor Thurow wanted to be stark, blunt and unmistakable. Those countries he was writing about were broke and he wanted to say so. If formal English has no truly fitting word for this sorry state of affairs, then let's forget about formal English.

Broke in the sense of *penniless* has of course a centuries-old history. It appeared in Samuel Pepys's diary in 1665 and has been used millions of times since then.

It means acute, painful financial misery.

brownie points. Reporting on an incident when the Reagan Administration leaked information to the *New*

York Times, the *New Republic* (9/6/82) wrote: "The Administration gets brownie points with the *Times's* brass."

What are brownie points? Well, a Brownie, as you possibly know, is a junior Girl Scout. Brownies get merit points whenever they've performed a good deed.

Now translate this system into a grownup organization, public or private. It's a fact of life that you earn "brownie points" by "obsequious behavior and flattering your superiors," as the *Dictionary of American Slang* says.

I ought to add that *Webster's New World Dictionary* says the whole business of brownie points is a myth. The idea that Girl Scouts get merit points is an "erroneous notion," it says. Maybe so. But *brownie points* is now firmly entrenched in the language. The phrase is always used with utter skepticism. *Random House* says they're "gained by servility, opportunism, or the like."

buff.   Around 1920, New York City volunteer firemen wore buff uniforms. That was the origin of the word *buff,* which now means any kind of fan or devotee. We have trolley-car buffs, Civil War buffs, police buffs, antique-car buffs, what-have-you.

What's new is that buffs have now made their amateurish way into high technology and high culture. *Time* (1/3/83) reported on a computer show in Las Vegas that was attended by "some 50,000 buyers, middlemen and assorted technology buffs." And the *New York Times* music critic John Rockwell wrote (12/30/82) about a performance of Bach's Brandenburg concertos, "To judge from Tuesday's performances, the Bach buffs are getting their money's worth."

Technology buffs? Bach buffs? Are serious students of computers or baroque music now treated as the same kind of people as fire watchers and railroad nuts? Is nothing sacred anymore? Has egalitarianism gone too far?

I think this common attitude of ours is refreshing. It's the gospel of upward mobility, transferred to high technology and culture. Anybody can be a computer buff if he gets a little home computer and learns the rules. Anyone can be a Bach buff if he gets hold of a tape recorder and a handful of cheap cassettes.

The pioneers used to be jacks-of-all-trades. Now we're all buffs.

bum idea.   What's the difference between a *bum* idea and a *bad* idea?

I ran across the phrase *bum idea* twice in recent months.

First *Newsweek* columnist Meg Greenfield (8/9/82) wrote about the proposed amendment to the Constitution that requires a balanced budget. She called it a "bum idea."

A few months later (1/9/83) Washington columnist James Reston of the *New York Times* wrote: "Maybe, as many people here believe, the notion of a Reagan-Andropov informal meeting is a bum idea."

Both Greenfield and Reston used the phrase *bum idea* rather than *bad idea.* Why? To find the answer, I looked up *bum* in all my dictionaries.

Bum, it turned out, comes from the German word *bummel,* which means a stroll. You *bummel* when you wander around aimlessly, loaf, loiter, idle, enjoy life at random. That's why a *bum* is a tramp, a hobo, a vagrant, a shiftless and irresponsible person.

Because of that basic meaning of *bum,* a *bum steer* is a direction given with no firm base, idly and arbitrarily. A *bum rap* is an accusation without evidence, with no facts to support it.

And a *bum idea* is not just a bad idea, rating one on a scale of one to ten. It's an *irresponsible* idea, an idea whose consequences have not been thought through, an idle, useless play of the mind.

Don't avoid the phrase *bum idea* just because it's slang. It's an excellent, quite indispensable term. The English language would be poorer without it.

bumping.   At the beginning of 1983, the U.S. Senate played a game of musical chairs. Senator Stennis of Mississippi gave up his ranking spot on the Armed Services Committee and claimed the ranking spot on the Appropriations Committee. When he did this, the *New York Times* reported (1/28/83) that "he bumped Senator William Proxmire, Democrat of Wisconsin."

Senator Proxmire, bereft of his ranking seat on Appropriations, promptly reclaimed his ranking spot on the Banking Committee. "In the process," the *Times* said, "he bumped Senator Donald W. Riegle Jr. of Michigan."

Bumping in the sense of displacing someone from a job— or from an airplane reservation—is a slang word, but that didn't bother the *Times*. It was the exact word for what went on, and was obviously the word to use.

The game of musical chairs among Senators may seem amusing, until you consider the consequences of those cute parliamentary moves. Senator Stennis is expected to use his new position to get funds for the completion of the Tennessee-Tombigbee Waterway in Mississippi. Senator Proxmire will lose his opportunities for getting federal money for highways and dams in Wisconsin. Senator Riegle will be less helpful to Michigan banks.

History is made not only by battles or elections. It's also made by bumping.

buttinsky.   In a column about consultants *(New York Times*, 2/22/83) Sydney Schanberg wrote, "The demand for outside recommenders, prescribers, proposers, idea-pushers and general buttinskies is so intense that the jobless problem may soon be all but solved."

A *buttinsky*, says *Webster's Collegiate*, is "one given to butting in: a troublesome meddler."

Where that lovely word comes from is unknown. It *is* known, though, that in 1902, George Ade, the great American humorist, wrote: "The Friend belonged to the Buttinsky Family and refused to stay on the Far Side of the Room."

He was followed in 1922 by Sinclair Lewis, who wrote in *Babbitt:* "If you think I'm a buttinsky, then I'll just butt in."

Then, in 1933, Dorothy Sayers wrote in *Murder Must Advertise:* "I never met with such a bunch of buttinskis. . . . Nothing is sacred to you."

This was followed in 1960 by P. G. Wodehouse, who wrote in *Jeeves in the Offing:* "It is never pleasant for a man of sensibility to find himself regarded as a buttinsky and a trailing arbutus."

buy.   In an article on House Speaker Tip O'Neill *(New Republic*, 1/24/83) I came across the sentence "He does not buy the notion that Reagan's victory was a mandate for reaction."

Buy in the sense of accept or believe is pure slang. It's about fifty years old. In a 1944 article in the linguistic journal *American Speech* a researcher explained: "If the work is perfect, the inspector *buys* it. . . . In the drilling departments one might hear a worker say, 'I'm waiting for the company to buy this hole.'"

By 1949 the usage had become general. *Time* magazine wrote, "After talking it over with the President . . . Secretary Johnson bought the Air Force point of view."

Like so many other popular usages, this use of *buy* to mean "accept an argument" is seemingly illogical. In theory, when we accept or reject an argument, we do it on its merits. If we're convinced that the argument is based on facts and convincing evidence, we accept it; if not, we say no.

But of course popular wisdom knows better. We buy an argument because we have been talked into it, or because it suits our prejudices, or for other trivial or irrelevant reasons.

Buying an argument usually is impulse buying.

chiseling.   Today (12/17/82) the *New York Times* ran an editorial entitled "Chiseling on the Poor." It dealt with the directors appointed by President Reagan to wreck legal services for the poor. They had not only tried hard to accomplish their nasty assignment, but billed the government sizable amounts for their services. For instance, Prof. William Harvey, the supposedly unpaid chairman of the Legal Services Corporation, had charged $25,000 for consultant services in 1982.

In its rightful indignation, the *Times* used the slang word *chiseling* to describe the outrage. There just isn't any better word for this kind of thing. *Chisel,* of course, means a tool for chipping away at wood or stone. Therefore, the verb *to chisel* means to *chip away,* whether at a marble statue or someone else's money. It's a particularly mean, niggling way of cheating, defrauding someone of small amounts in an underhanded way.

The *Times* editorial quoted a Congressman who said the directors of the Legal Services Corporation "put all four feet and a snout into the trough."

chortle.   *Chortle* is one of the handful of English words that can be traced back to a specific person who coined it at a specific date. It was invented by Lewis Carroll, the author of *Alice in Wonderland,* and appeared for the first time in the famous "Jabberwocky" poem in the book *Through the Looking Glass* (1871). The last stanza read:

> *"And hast thou slain the Jabberwock?*
> *Come to my arms, my beamish boy!*
> *O frabjous day! Callooh! Callay!"*
> *He chortled in his joy.*

Writing these unforgettable lines, Carroll gave us the lovely word *chortle,* which you'll find duly listed in all dictionaries. Obviously he made it up by combining *chuckle* and *snort.* Someone who chortles is half-chuckling, half-snorting—an infrequent but not wholly unknown way of expressing your feelings.

So there we have this excellent expression—and we don't use it. Only once in a long while, if you're an assiduous reader, you'll find it in print, as I did in Sydney Schanberg's column (*New York Times,* 12/7/82). Granted, he used *chortle* in an imaginary dialogue with his friend Trafalgar, but it shouldn't be too difficult to work in the word *chortle* on other occasions.

Whenever you interview someone, keep your ears open and try to catch your interviewee in the act of chortling. When he does, be sure to put it down.

Let's make more use of Lewis Carroll's great gift to the English language.

chummy.   On December 20, 1982, the U.S. Secretary of State George Shultz and the French Foreign Minister Claude Cheysson gave a joint press conference in Paris. The *New York Times* foreign affairs columnist Flora Lewis was amazed by their informality. "The press conference," she wrote, "oozed chummy affection. They took turns answering questions, calling each other Claude and George. . . ."

I looked up *chummy* in the major dictionaries. They called the word "informal" or "colloquial" and defined it as "friendly, intimate, sociable." Three rather formal words to define an informal one.

The thought occurred to me that our whole system of dictionarymaking is upside down. You go to the dictionary because you want to know the meaning of an unfamiliar word. The dictionary then translates the word into a string of even more unfamiliar words. For instance, if you're not sure what *larkspur* means, *Webster's Collegiate* will tell you, "any of a genus (*Delphinium*) of plants of the buttercup family; *esp:* a cultivated annual delphinium grown for its showy irregular flowers with spurred calyxes." You then look up *calyx* and find: "the external usu. green or leafy part of a flower consisting of sepals." You next look up *sepal* and find: "one of the modified leaves comprising a calyx." At that point you give up.

Wouldn't it be better to use familiar words to explain the *un*familiar ones?

chutzpah. Writing about a recent OPEC meeting, Charles Krauthammer (*New Republic*, 2/21/83) said, "The Saudi oil minister, Sheik Yamani, set the tone for the debate on whether the imminent collapse of the Organization of Petroleum Exporting Countries is good or bad. With characteristic chutzpah he declared: 'Everybody needs OPEC, even the consumers.'"

Why did Krauthammer use the Yiddish slang word *chutzpah?* Because standard English has no word meaning gigantic, unbelievable impudence—the kind that can call a cartel that's raised the price of a barrel of oil from $2.50 to $34 "good for consumers."

Dictionaries have struggled for years to define *chutzpah*, but have fallen woefully short. They say "impudence," "nerve," "gall," but none of those words comes anywhere near the breathtaking size of *chutzpah*. *Random House* has "unmitigated effrontery," *American Heritage* has "brazenness," *Webster's Collegiate* has "supreme self-confidence," *Webster's New World* has "shameless audacity."

The last two definitions *almost* catch the impossible, against-all-odds flavor of *chutzpah*, but of course they can't. Only the Jews, fighting for sheer survival for two thousand years, could arrive at the concept of true chutzpah.

classy.   At the occasion of President Reagan's New Year visit to Palm Springs, California, the *New York Times* (12/31/82) ran a piece about the place. It said that "it evolved from being an exclusive enclave of the very rich to a resort for the upper middle class and the newly rich."

A local restaurateur told the *Times* reporter, "I liked it better in the old days. Before, they were the very wealthy, classy people. . . ."

Classy didn't always mean the same as very wealthy. The *Random House Dictionary* defines *classy* as "of high class, rank, or grade; stylish; admirable." And the *Supplement to the Oxford English Dictionary* gives quotes going back to the 1890s, none of which says anything about wealth. For instance, the English novelist Eden Philpotts wrote in 1899, "He said a man who sold pills and toothbrushes . . . could not be considered a classy chemist."

It's a far cry from that Victorian concept of *classy* to the idea that very wealthy people are classy simply because they've got a lot of money.

The word *classy* is no longer very classy.

clout.   The word *clout* has been part of the English language for centuries. It has many meanings. It means a piece of cloth, a cuff on the head, a target in archery, a baseball hit.

Suddenly, in the 1960s, a new meaning became popular. *Clout* now is the favorite word for political influence.

The *Wall Street Journal,* in a review of the book *Sez Who? Sez Me* by the Chicago columnist Mike Royko (12/30/82), says: "Mr. Royko takes his readers on tours of the seamy underworld of clout. He tells of a downtown luncheonette, where lawyers and judges, bagmen and aldermen gather to cut deals . . . 'Many of the customers seemed to communicate solely by winking, nodding, and passing unmarked envelopes.'"

Those days are long gone. Clout has come out of the closet. Elected and appointed officials are rated on their amount of clout. The *New York Times* (11/17/82) wrote about the President's Council of Economic Advisers: "What clout it has had in recent years has been attributable mainly to the force and personality of some individual chairmen." And a long article in the *New York Times Magazine* (12/12/82) was called "The Clout of the 'New' Bob Dole." It analyzed in detail the political power of Senator Bob Dole, chairman of the Senate Finance Committee.

So the slang word *clout,* once an underworld term for under-the-table deals, has risen to become the standard term for political influence and power.

Soon we'll see a new stage in our political life. Just as our Presidents are subjected to monthly popular-approval ratings in the polls, so the clout of *all* government officials will regularly be rated. Being elected or appointed is no longer enough —now your effectiveness in your job goes up and down like a yo-yo.

Leave it to the social scientists to find a way to measure and quantify clout.

comeuppance. In *The New Yorker* (1/10/83) Pauline Kael described a recent movie in which "bigoted whites . . . get their comeuppance from the bitingly clever black man."

Comeuppance is a lovely, very American word, built from the common phrase *come up* and the Latin ending *-ance.* It means deserved punishment or retribution.

Comeuppance was first used in print in 1859. It was used several times by the classic American novelist William Dean Howells. In 1943 the historian D. W. Brogan wrote, "The roles of teacher and taught were suddenly reversed, to the delight of a world that saw the English at last get their comeuppance."

Comeuppance, with its folksy dialect roots, describes neatly the delight of the underdog when he gets his revenge.

Justice doesn't always triumph, and when it does, you need a word that expresses the elation you feel. *Retribution* is much too formal and solemn. It has that awed feeling of the mysterious workings of fate. *Comeuppance* is more down to earth. It sounds like something that happens naturally, in the ordinary course of events.

Or so we hope.

comfy. Can you use the word *comfy* in writing?
The New Yorker's "Talk of the Town" column did it recently

(1/10/83). It quoted "a young stockbroker friend" who wrote: "I am leaving Wall Street soon after the first of the year for the West Coast. Now, the thing is how to adapt without quite leaving my comfy Northeast self behind. . . ."

Comfy is a pleasant "colloquial" word listed in all dictionaries. Of course, it's a shortened form of *comfortable,* and no wonder. *Comfortable* just isn't a comfortable word to pronounce, what with four syllables and seven consonants. The British deal with this kind of word by disregarding all vowels and saying *kmftbl,* but we Americans don't go for this approach. We rather say *comfy* and feel comfy about it.

In case you wonder whether the word should be confined to the nursery or at least to strictly feminine usage, relax. It's been used since 1829—among others by the following definitely male writers:

Rudyard Kipling: "Put to bed on some rolled-up carpets, all comfy."

Edgar Wallace: "I'm in London, which is delightfully capitalistic and comfy."

Walter de la Mare: "Let's sit down here comfily on the stones."

You may also refer to the 1969 Sears, Roebuck Catalogue: "Crochet-look tights. Comfy, elastic weights."

con man. The *Oxford English Dictionary* has an elaborate explanation of *confidence trick:* "a method of professional swindling, in which the victim is induced to hand over money or other valuables as a token of 'confidence' in the sharper." A *confidence man* is then defined, citing an example from the 1880s, as "one who practises this trick; a professional swindler of respectable appearance and address."

A hundred years have passed since those idyllic days. Confidence men soon became so common that the word had to be shortened to *con man.* And the simple confidence game practiced in Victorian England changed into a thousand forms of scams and elaborate swindles. The slang word *con man* became so widely known and used that it was applied, according to the *Dictionary of American Slang,* to "anyone who earns money easily" or "any handsome charming male."

Today *con man* is used for anyone who commits a fraud, whether criminal or not. In *The New Yorker* (1/24/83), Jane Kramer wrote about the late President de Gaulle of France: "De Gaulle believed that the world would end with him—and France—sitting out the apocalypse. He was a con man on a grand scale."

That's a far cry from the small-time swindler "of respectable appearance and address."

contact. The other day (11/2/82) the *New York Times* ran a piece on a controversial alcoholism study. "The one major failure found by the committee," the *Times* wrote, "was that the Sobells [a husband-and-wife research team] did not contact the subjects every month, as they had said they had, to check up on drinking."

Contact, used as a verb, has been the bugaboo of purists for many decades. Why they hate it so isn't clear—probably because the word was invented by business-letter writers rather than academics.

Anyway, *contact* has become the test case of the "correct usage" fans, right behind the famous *hopefully.*

The 1962 edition of the *New York Times* stylebook said simply: *"contact.* Do not use as a verb."

The world and the dictionaries paid no attention to that prissy edict. Everybody uses *contact* as a verb every day, and all major dictionaries, except the diehard *American Heritage,* now accept the usage without a murmur.

Came 1976 and the *Times* style manual was revised. Grudgingly, the new *New York Times Manual of Style and Usage* retreated an inch or two: *"contact* (v.). Although it has gained acceptance, it remains graceless and has also achieved triteness. On those grounds, avoid it where possible."

As you see, *Times* writers prefer to be graceless and trite. Follow their enlightened example.

contraption. The *New York Times* (11/2/82) reported on the popularity of small electric appliances. Suburban stores, the paper said, were full of peanut butter makers, pizza keepers, salad dryers, orange juice squeezers with pulp ejectors, Bread Brain toasters, and Smart Irons. "You come in looking for something simple," one shopper was quoted as saying, "and you walk out with some incredible contraption."

Contraption is a lovely 19th-century word. The *Oxford English Dictionary* defines *contraption* as a contrivance or device (with suggestion of ingenuity rather than effectiveness). *Webster's Third* says "a newfangled or complicated device— usu. used in mild scorn or indulgence."

Between the two definitions, there emerges a surprising truth. When we call something a contraption, we realize that it doesn't work very well or may soon go kaput, but that's exactly why we're rather fond of the damn thing. It's a lovable problem child. It has its faults, God knows, but look how cleverly it's put together.

And after all, that mildly ridiculous contraption may be a work of genius. The Wright brothers at Kitty Hawk flew in what may rightly be called a contraption, and many of Edison's early models were much the same kind of thing. But he lit up the world, and the Wright brothers made us fly.

It wasn't done with mirrors, it was done with contraptions.

cop. The official *New York Times Manual of Style and Usage* (1976) says *Webster's New World Dictionary* is to be used as the authority for spelling and definitions. "But," it adds, *"New World* provides a great deal more information concerning whether a word is slang, informal, colloquial, substandard or vulgar."

When it comes to the word *cop, Times* staff members know where to look. The *New World Dictionary* says that *cop* the verb, meaning "to seize, capture, win, steal, etc.," is slang. So is *cop* the noun, meaning a policeman.

But the *Times* of 1982 pays little attention to its authoritative dictionary. On November 5, 1982, the word *cop* appeared three times in its pages. Page B2 carried a headline "Direct Line to a Cop," over an article dealing with phone calls to local precincts. A few pages later, there was a theater review dealing with a new play by Murray Schisgal, about two neighbors—a policewoman and an out-of-work actor. "The cop," the reviewer wrote, ". . . is skeptical of all men." Later on, in the TV program, a movie is summarized this way: "Ex-cop hired to seek a supposedly missing woman."

Cop has a very ironical history. The verb *to cop* originally was thieves' slang, and meant "to catch, nab, steal, filch." Then the thieves began applying their slang word to the police and called the policemen "coppers"—that is, people whose job it was to catch thieves. Finally, "copper" was abbreviated to "cop" and began to be used by ordinary, non-criminal citizens.

The turnaround of the despised enemy of the criminal to the hero of society took some two hundred years. At first the highwayman or robber was the hero, and the policeman was an object of scorn. (The definition of "policeman" in the *Oxford English Dictionary* is "a paid constable.") Then, with the rise of the detective story, the sleuth on the side of law and order became a hero—but it was the private detective, never the policeman, who was the great admired hero. There's a long line from Poe's Auguste Dupin to Conan Doyle's Sherlock Holmes to Agatha Christie's Hercule Poirot and Rex Stout's Nero Wolfe—two, three generations of private detectives who bring criminals to justice while the police bumble and fumble. At last, over a generation ago, the policeman became recognized as a hero and the word *cop* emerged from slang and reached the height of respectability.

copout. As I just said, the verb *to cop* was originally thieves' slang for "to catch, nab, steal, filch." Then how did the word *copout* get its present meaning?

The connection is clear when you look at an earlier form of *cop out,* which was "cop *an* out." In other words, someone who cops out grabs a chance to get out. He cops a plea to get out from under a harsher punishment, he escapes, he stops working or gets away from society altogether. If he's in a bind, or embarrassing situation, he compromises, evades the issue or retreats from reality.

The *Dictionary of American Slang* defines *cop out* this way: "to renege or withdraw from involvement . . . to evade a question . . . to break a promise; to compromise or abandon one's ideals, principles, etc."

God knows there's enough of all this going on in this world, and within a few years the word *copout* has become one of the most widely used words in our language.

Newsweek, in a review of a recent movie about lesbianism, says (2/7/83): "One is struck . . . by the errors the movie avoids: [it] simply refuses to indulge in any of the usual Hollywood copouts that accompany this terrain. There are no breast-beating melodramatics, evasions, special pleading."

Copout is an indispensable word.

corny.   Mimi Sheraton, the restaurant critic of the *New York Times*, had a terrible day (1/14/83). Luchow's, the famous old German restaurant, had moved uptown from 14th Street to Broadway and she'd gone to eat dinner at the new location. It was simply awful.

The sauerkraut had a "musty boardinghouse" taste. The duck and goose were "stringy and reheated." The braised veal shank was "of the type one might expect on a hospital tray." The schnitzels were "soggy." The beefsteak was "tough." The pecan-breaded shrimp "smelled of iodine."

Sheraton ended her report with the sentence: "Even at $16.95, the pretheater dinner seems overpriced, especially when either the corny brass band or the string and piano trio blasts away."

Now really! An old-fashioned German brass band is *supposed* to be corny. *Corny* means "unsophisticated, old-fashioned, trite, banal, sentimental, mawkish, lacking in subtlety and full of clichés, dated, melodramatic, hackneyed, repeated so often that people get tired of it."

That's what the dictionaries say. But aren't they a little biased? Wentworth and Flexner's *Dictionary of American Slang* says about *corny:* "Originally pejorative . . . now in general use, though beginning to become archaic." Which means, to my mind, that *corny* now means old-fashioned, but is widely used with a fond, indulgent smile.

In a country where country and western music is vastly popular and where some 90 percent of the daily TV fare is pure corn, the word *corny* has long ceased to be a term of contempt.

Mimi Sheraton was entitled to find the food abominable, but she should have left the German band alone. They were doing their corny best.

cough up, shell out, fork over, plunk down.   Not long ago (10/25/82), *Newsweek* reported that shoppers now "cough up about 18.5 percent annual interest on revolving credit lines."

A few weeks later, the *New York Times* (11/2/82) referred to Lew Lehrman, who was "on his way to shelling out well over $11 million . . . in pursuit of the Governor's chair."

Some time after that, *The New Yorker* (11/22/82) published its annual piece on Christmas gifts for women. It started this way: "Before we take another step, we'll march straight into the stationery department of Bloomingdale's and fork over $2.50 for two sheets of gift-wrap paper printed all over with outsize hundred-dollar bills."

Finally (12/11/82) there was a book review in the *Nation.* It contained this phrase: "When you plunk down your $5 for a [movie] ticket . . ."

Why does the English language have so many slang substitutes for the simple word *pay?* That's an intriguing question, which leaves room for all kinds of speculation.

My own answer is that people resent the necessity of spending money. The whole business of paying, paying, paying for everything is a confounded nuisance. Let's not mention the subject; let's camouflage it.

creep.   What is a creep? A creep, of course, is someone who gives you the creeps. And what are the creeps? Accord-

ing to the *Random House Dictionary,* "a sensation of horror, fear, disgust, etc., suggestive of the feeling induced by something crawling over the skin."

The earliest appearance of the creeps in print was in 1849, in Dickens's *David Copperfield.* There Mrs. Gummidge "was constantly complaining of the cold, and of its occasioning a visitation in her back which she called 'the creeps.'"

Human creeps have appeared in print since 1876. At first a creep was the real thing, a person who gave you that gruesome, insect-crawling feeling. But gradually *creep* became a more general word of contempt, with certain unpleasant overtones. P. G. Wodehouse wrote in 1954, "They were creeps of the first water and would bore the pants off me."

Creep is slang, of course, which doesn't stop it from appearing in the *New York Times.* A classic example was a comment from a runner in the New York City 1982 Marathon about Alberto Salazar, the winner. "Salazar is a creep. He's bionic. They shouldn't let nonhumans in the race."

A few days later the movie critic Janet Maslin wrote about the growing violence in horror movies. "There is no opportunity to view the monster as the embodiment of a community's fears, or as the darker side of man's nature, or as anything other than a cryptic, single-minded creep."

It's a waste of a splendid word to call just any boring no-account a creep. There are enough of the really creepy kind of creeps around.

crummy. In an interview in the *New Republic* (12/13/82) Congressman Barber Conable was talking about political action committees. "These new PACs," he said, "not only buy incumbents, but affect legislation. It's the same crummy business as judges putting the arm on lawyers who appear before them to finance their next campaign."

Crummy, of course, is derived from *crumb.* Basically, it means brittle, ready to break into crumbs, and therefore no good. It's labeled slang in most dictionaries, and defined as "dirty, cheap, shabby, disgusting, inferior, worthless, contemptible."

One dictionary defines it as "lousy." That got me thinking. Do *crummy* and *lousy* really mean the same thing?

I think not. The behavior of judges and politicians who can be influenced by money is crummy, but it isn't exactly lousy. *Crummy* refers to a moral or aesthetic defect, *lousy* means disgusting and contemptible in general. Much that goes on in social life is *crummy,* but not necessarily *lousy.* You can say "I'm feeling lousy," but you wouldn't say "I'm feeling crummy," unless you're ashamed of something you've done.

cute.   The word *cute* in the sense of attractive or charming goes back to the 1830s. Originally it was an abbreviation of the word *acute,* which means shrewd or sharp-witted. But gradually the sense of wit and cleverness faded away and only the general charm and attractiveness remained. The *New York Times* (1/2/83) told about a female Dartmouth student who was using her computer terminal to chat electronically with a male colleague. She found out where he was on the campus, ran over and looked at him, ran back and typed "You're cute." Surely she couldn't have formed an opinion about his mental capacities.

Lately the word *cute* has taken on a negative meaning. People began to realize that cuteness is often manufactured and carefully contrived. So cuteness got a bad name. The unabridged *Webster's Third* lists a new meaning: "obviously straining for effect: mawkish through affected archness, prettiness or contrivance."

"TRB" in the *New Republic* wrote about former Vice-President Mondale. He'd been asked on "Meet the Press" whether he was running for the presidency. "I saw no reason to be cute about it," he said, "and I said yes, I was."

So use the word *cute* if you want to, but watch out. It's a double-edged sword.

damn.   In an interview in the *New York Times* (12/22/82) Robert McNamara, the retired head of the World Bank, talked about his present life.

He complained that he could no longer run up eleven flights of stairs to his office as he did at the World Bank.

"They won't let me run up the damn stairs. The doors are locked, top and bottom, so I can't do it."

Why did McNamara damn the stairs? No reason except just a little added emphasis. *Damn*—or *damned*—is a word that has fallen on bad days. The definition in the *Random House Dictionary* reads: "1. condemned or doomed, esp. to eternal punishment. 2. detestable; loathsome. 3. utter: *a damned fool.*"

You can see the steep decline in the power of the word. It has been totally washed out and is now a meaningless little flourish.

Damn, the lighthearted throwaway adjective or adverb, is quite common nowadays. Meg Greenfield in *Newsweek* (7/12/82) wrote, "Politicians are heard to say they will not be intimidated by the Israeli lobby but will vote and act as they damn please." Pauline Kael in *The New Yorker* (10/4/82) wrote, "The plot is just one damn thing after another going wrong for the boys."

Does this mean you should cut out all those unnecessary *damns* you use in your speech or writing? Not at all. They don't mean anything anymore. That's exactly why you should use them.

A little *damn* now and then adds flavor and zest.

data.   An article on faked research in the *New York Times* (12/27/82) said, "Dr. Cort reported data on that work that was different from the data the committee found in his laboratory notebooks."

Purists jump to the ceiling when they see *data* with a singular verb, but the American people couldn't care less. Never mind the *New York Times Manual of Style and Usage* (1976), which says, "data (pl.)"; never mind *The Elements of Style* by Strunk and White (3d ed. 1979), which says, "Like *strata, phenomena,* and *media, data* is a plural"; never mind the *Oxford American Dictionary* (1980), which says, "data should not be used with a singular verb"; never mind the *American Heritage Dictionary* (2d ed. 1982), which says, "*data* . . . traditionally takes a plural verb."

And never mind the famous first edition of Fowler's *Modern English Usage* (1926), which says, "*data* is plural only (*The data are,* not *is, insufficient*)."

I don't blame Fowler for his total disregard of popular usage. After all, he was an old scholar, steeped in Latin and Greek, who wrote about the silent *p* in *pneumatic* and *pneumonia,* "It is to be hoped that these silent letters may recover their voices now that everyone can read."

But our current purists ought to know better. They seem to live in a fairyland where everyone is bilingual in English and Latin practically from birth and feels a physical twinge of pain whenever "the data was" appears on a printed page.

deadbeat.   In a front-page article on credit card frauds, the *Wall Street Journal* (1/24/83) said, "In the 1970s, many banks indiscriminately mailed out credit cards to increase market share and ended up with a lot of deadbeat customers."

What is a *deadbeat?* A hundred years ago, the word meant, according to the *Oxford English Dictionary,* "a worthless idler who sponges on his friends; a sponger, loafer." Bret Harte in 1884 wrote about "every tramp and deadbeat you've met."

During the 19th century the meaning of *deadbeat* gradually changed. By 1966, when the unabridged *Random House Dictionary* appeared, its definition read: "1. a person who deliberately avoids paying his debts. 2. a loafer, sponger." Sixteen years later, the *American Heritage Dictionary* (2d ed.) came out. Its definition read: "1. A person who does not pay his debts. 2. A lazy person; loafer."

You see what happened? The *Random House* definition still says "deliberately." The *American Heritage* definition does not.

The change is now complete. A hundred years ago a deadbeat was someone like a tramp or a hobo. Now he's simply someone who doesn't pay what he owes the bank. The computer doesn't care about morals or motives: a person who doesn't pay is a deadbeat. Period.

deep-six.   Writing about the Israeli report on the Beirut massacre (2/10/83), *New York Times* columnist William Safire said, "The independent commission's verdict stands in contrast with Lebanon's own deep-sixed investigation of those guilty of the massacre."

"Deep-sixed"! For those of us who who lived through the Watergate scandals this is an intensely nostalgic word. Those

were the days when high government officials were casually talking about destroying evidence by throwing it over the bridge into the Potomac River. Safire, like all of us, remembers and uses the word where it clearly fits—for the never-publicized report of the Lebanese government.

Deep-six is a slang word having to do with burial at sea under six fathoms of water. Its appearance without quotation marks in the *New York Times* is something of a landmark. Of course, you might say that columnists of the stature of William Safire have special privileges. But I don't think so. The simple truth is that the *Times,* faced with the onrush of slang, has thrown in the towel.

There's hardly a slangier word than *deep-six.* It reminds you simultaneously of the criminal underworld *and* of corruption in government.

deli.   *The New Yorker* is probably the most stylized magazine in the United States. At times its never-ending sentences are downright bizarre. Consider this, from Andy Logan's City Hall report (10/11/82): "Inside City Hall—the two-and-a-half-story Renaissance palace, completed in 1812, that Henry James called 'the divine . . . the elegant, the gallant little structure,' and that comes as a revelation to many out-of-towners, who think all New York buildings that aren't slum housing are chrome-plated skyscrapers—everything was quiet on Primary Day, as is often true when the head of a house is off somewhere." Sixty-three words.

But *The New Yorker* style is so fine that it can even overcome such blemishes. All staff writers are trained to use informal or even slang words wherever they fit to balance any heavy spots.

The next sentence after Miss Logan's reference to Henry

James reads: "At the foot of City Hall's steps, shortly after noon, Richard Iacona's Bad Little Big Band was playing Gershwin tunes while workers in the area—municipal employees and others—sat about on the marble steps eating their deli sandwiches and swaying their shoulders to the music."

It's the informal little word *deli* that provides the saving grace here. Of course, some of those step-sitters may have munched homemade, brown-bag sandwiches, but many had indeed bought their pastrami or salami from a nearby delicatessen.

Miss Logan knew exactly what she was writing about. The simple word *deli* added the genuine New York touch.

ding-a-ling.   In *The New Yorker* (1/10/83) Pauline Kael briefly reviewed the George Bernard Shaw movie *Caesar and Cleopatra* in which Vivien Leigh played Cleopatra. "It's lucky," she wrote, "that Leigh has such an amusing ding-a-ling quality."

When it comes to *ding-a-ling* and *dingbat,* the dictionaries are in a state of hopeless confusion.

Let's start with *ding-a-ling.* For almost a century, this word has been used to imitate the sound of a bell. Then, around 1960, *ding-a-ling* began to be used for a person who was crazy, eccentric, a screwball. *Webster's New World Dictionary* says this has to do with "the ringing in the head of a punch-drunk boxer." No other dictionary agrees.

Now let's look at *dingbat.* It has several meanings, which seem to have no connection with each other. It means (1) money, (2) anything that can be thrown, (3) a gadget or dingus, (4) a muffin, biscuit, or bun, (5) a hobo, (6) an Italian, (7) a Chinese, (8) a decorative device in printing.

Then came the "All in the Family" TV series that used *ding-bat* as a general insult, mainly meaning stupid.

By now, I'm afraid, *dingbat* has replaced the lovely word *ding-a-ling*. The 1982 *American Heritage Dictionary* has the following two entries:

> ding-a-ling. *A silly person; dingbat.*
> dingbat. *1. A small object . . . suitable for hurling. . . . 2. A typographical ornament. . . . 3. A silly or foolish person. [Orig. unknown]*

dipsy-doodle.

On November 16, 1982, President Reagan gave a formal speech before a meeting of the United States League of Savings Associations in New Orleans.

The speech was duly reported in the media, including the *New York Times.* A high point was this passage: "A propaganda campaign would have you believe these deficits are caused by our so-called massive tax cut and defense buildup. Well, that's a real dipsy-doodle because, even after our tax deductions are fully in place, they will barely neutralize the enormous payroll tax increases approved in 1977."

What's a *dipsy-doodle?* The word is so slangy that it isn't listed in any of the four major desk dictionaries—*Webster's Collegiate, Random House College, Webster's New World* and *American Heritage.* I finally tracked it down in Wentworth and Flexner's *Dictionary of American Slang* (2d ed. 1975). There it is duly listed as "1. Chicanery, deception. 2. In baseball, a sharp curved pitch."

What have we here? The President of the United States in a formal speech before a formal audience of bankers uses a term that is so slangy you can't find it in any major dictionary. Did it just slip out, a remembered term from his youthful days as a sports announcer? No way. This was not an off-the-cuff campaign speech—it was given two weeks after the election—but a carefully prepared formal address, probably the work of a platoon of speechwriters. They decided that *dipsy-doodle* was just the right word to use in addressing the bankers. Aggressive and yet homey, a sharp attack on the opposition with disarming baseball overtones.

What does this do to the doctrine of correct English and the taboo on slang in formal language?

I say the whole thing is a dipsy-doodle.

discombobulate. Pauline Kael, *The New Yorker* movie critic, recently (11/29/82) wrote about a movie in which two women check out men as possible fathers for a baby. "Those four blue eyes," Kael wrote, "are very discombobulating to the men they stare at."

Congratulations to Pauline Kael for using the nice old word *discombobulate.* It's a 150-year-old joke, but it's still fresh and entertaining and ought to be used more often. We don't have so many whimsical inventions in our language that we can afford to pass them by.

Discombobulate is a play on the word *discomfit* or maybe *discompose.* The dictionaries aren't sure which; nor do they know who coined the word. It means disconcert or make uneasy.

Now the funny thing is that the word *discomfit*—which is the non-slang synonym of *discombobulate*—is itself a bone of contention between the purists and the scientific linguists. The purists say that *discomfit* means utterly defeat in battle, and that people "erroneously" use *discomfit* when they mean *discomfort.* They say it does *not* mean making someone uncomfortable. The linguists say that popular usage must be given its head and *discomfit* is a perfectly fine word for making someone uneasy.

My advice is, use *discombobulate* and avoid the whole argument.

disinvite. In *The New Yorker* (2/7/83) William F. Buckley published a journal he'd kept during a recent period. He wrote that he'd invited the harpsichordist Rosalyn Tureck to a staff Christmas party at the *National Review,* but was asked by the performing musician not to let her come. "So, rather apprehensively, I asked Frances to call Rosalyn's secretary and gently disinvite her."

I checked *disinvite* in the four major desk dictionaries. It wasn't there. Then I checked the unabridged *Random House Dictionary.* Nothing. I then checked the unabridged *Webster's Third* and found this one-line entry:

> *disinvite* vt [dis-+ invite] obs: *to recall an invitation to*

Finally I went to the *Oxford English Dictionary.* I found *disinvite* listed as obsolete, with three quotes from the 16th and 17th centuries. End of search.

Does this mean that Buckley had whimsically dug up an obsolete word? Not at all. Being a professional writer, he'd made use of the potential of the English language. *Dis*— like *de, re, un,* and some others—is what's known as a live prefix. So, when he needed a word conveying the sense of canceling an invitation, he recoined the word *disinvite.* It's short, it's clear to everyone and it does the job.

English teachers have done their damnedest to make us timid when it comes to inventing or reinventing words. This book is meant to disintimidate you.

do a number on.   Soon after taking office, Governor Cuomo of New York announced new rules for his staff in dealing with the press (*New York Times,* 1/19/83): "Speak but speak prudently. Speak generously. Speak honestly. Speak without malice. Don't hurt. Don't take a cheap shot. Don't use anonymity to do a number on somebody."

Do a number on is very recent slang. It means "to disparage; speak or write with contempt or disrespect; hurt or harm; make fun of." The phrase didn't appear in print until 1974. Nobody knows exactly where it comes from.

The interesting thing about Governor Cuomo's directive was the extreme simplicity of its language. It was written that way because the governor was most anxious that it should be fully understood and obeyed. So he shied away from the usual kind of official gobbledygook and turned to almost biblical simplicity.

Not only that, he decided to use recent slang to make sure everybody knew what he meant. Note that the instructions say, "Don't hurt." Then they say, "Don't take a cheap shot," which means more or less the same thing. Then, to ram the point home, they say, "Don't do a number on somebody."

Purists always tell us not to use slang, particularly not in formal documents. What could be more formal than an official government directive with instructions that must be obeyed?

Governor Cuomo saw what was needed. If you want to make sure everyone understands what is meant, don't use formal English. Use slang.

dough.   The pun was irresistible. A California bakery chain had announced that it would soon open twenty cookie stores in New York. This called for an amusing editorial in the

New York Times (2/7/83). After mentioning Marcel Proust, no less, and extolling the delights of chocolate chip cookies, the writer said, "Though Manhattan streets are already awash in chocolate chip cookies, a West Coast cookie chain is betting a lot of dough on New Yorkers' infinite need for its special brand of comfort."

The slang word *dough,* in the sense of money, goes back to the 1850s. How and why the "mixture of flour, liquid and other ingredients worked into a soft, thick mass" was first used as a handy metaphor for money, we don't know. Anyway, it has been so used for almost one and a half centuries by many literary notables. P. G. Wodehouse, in his book *Money in the Bank* (1946), wrote, "She's got more dough than you could shake a stick at."

So don't hesitate if you want to use the venerable word *dough* in the sense of money. You may also use *bread, moolah, mazuma, jack, shekels, spondulicks, cabbage, lettuce, spinach, do-re-mi, loot, gravy, simoleons, wampum,* or just simply *bucks.*

Don't feel you have to stick to the boring word *money.* You can do better than that.

downer.   On December 27, 1982, *Newsweek* ran a trivia quiz on the past year. One question was: "Next year will be a downer for the Duke, Zonker and their friends. Why?" The answer was: "'Doonesbury' creator Garry Trudeau is taking a leave of absence."

The word *downer* is about a dozen years old. When it was first used, it meant a depressant drug, like a barbiturate, sedative or tranquilizer.

The first appearance of *downer* in print was in 1970. But the development of slang words sometimes is incredibly fast. In that same year, 1970, *downer* was also first used in print to mean a depressing experience. The words *downer, upper* and *bummer* were immediately picked up to be used in their metaphorical senses.

Today most dictionaries list a secondary meaning of *downer* that has nothing to do with drugs. A *downer* is simply "a depressing or negative experience, situation, predicament, person or thing"—just about anything that makes you feel bad.

My example from *Newsweek* goes a tiny bit further. It's an ironical use of the metaphorical meaning of *downer.* Surely, the year-long absence of a favorite comic strip is the mildest of depressants. Nothing like a barbiturate.

dumb.   In *Webster's New World Dictionary, dumb* is defined this way: "1. lacking the power of speech; mute 2. unwilling to talk; silent; reticent 3. not accompanied by speech 4. temporarily speechless, as from fear, grief, etc. 5. producing no sound 6. lacking some normal part, characteristic, or quality 7. [Colloq.] stupid; moronic; unintelligent."

Other dictionaries define *dumb* in much the same way. The meaning "stupid" is the last and least, grudgingly admitted.

Actually, *dumb* is now much more common in the sense of stupid than in the sense of mute. It's our normal word when we talk about someone's stupidity. Perhaps the reason is that our attitude has changed. To accuse someone of stupidity is pretty harsh; so we say *dumb,* which is a little gentler and implies that someone's lack of intelligence isn't their fault and is therefore forgivable. After all, a high IQ isn't everything.

Writing in the *New York Times* about phone-answering machines, Jean Kerr (12/29/82) quotes her friend Betsy: "The machine was perfect, perfect, but all our friends were so *dumb!*

Even though Bill distinctly said to wait for the beep, *nobody* waited for the beep."

Did Betsy mean that all their friends were stupid? She did not. They were just dumb—a little slow on the uptake.

dump on.   January 20, 1983, was the day of a breakthrough in the field of writing.

On that day the *New York Times* ran a full-page ad for *The New Yorker* magazine. The ad contained four excerpts from the current issue. One of them came from a movie review by Pauline Kael and said, "He [the movie director] appears to believe that a man of feeling is necessarily a weakling . . . who spends his life getting dumped on while worrying about justice in the abstract."

To *dump* means to defecate. This meaning of the word is not listed in any of the four major desk dictionaries. The *New York Times Everyday Dictionary* delicately defines *dump on* as "criticize harshly; harass verbally." The *Barnhart Dictionary of New English Since 1963*, equally delicately, defines it as "heckle."

The true meaning of *dump on* is given in the *Supplement to the Oxford English Dictionary* and in Wentworth and Flexner's *Dictionary of American Slang*. However, even Wentworth and Flexner label the word as "taboo."

Now *dump on* has appeared in *The New Yorker* and the *New York Times.*

I've read Pauline Kael's review, including the long-forbidden word. I can attest that the movie's main character, who lets his wife's lover sleep in his home and is being literally kicked in the pants on-screen, can fairly be described as being dumped on.

elephantine.   To give your reader a little extra pleasure, don't just rely on the current crop of slang and informal
words. Sometimes it's good to reach back for an ancient but
still amusing joke. The word *discombobulate,* for instance. Or
the word *elephantine.* Elephants have been around for many
thousands of years, but to compare something vast to an elephant is still a valid humorous metaphor.

In an article in the *New York Times Magazine* (3/6/83) Earl
C. Ravenal described some of the proposals to cut the $274
billion 1984 defense budget. Senator David F. Durenberger of
Minnesota, for instance, spent many months of labor in producing a 195-page scheme. He'd junk the Army's AH-64 helicopter and the Navy's F/A-18 fighter-bomber, replace nuclear
aircraft carriers with oil-fueled ones and cancel some elements of our continental air defense. "These elephantine labors, however, produced a fiscal mouse: $3 billion of cuts for
1982 and $27 billion to $55 billion over five years."

I looked up *elephantine* and found that it has rarely been
used to refer directly to elephants. But it has been used stead-
ily since 1845 in its metaphorical sense, always with a mildly
amusing effect.

So if you spot some elephantine labors producing a mouse,
say so.

enormity.   The English language has two words—
enormous and *enormity*—that present a little usage problem.

Enormous means huge, vast, of great size. *Enormity* means
great wickedness, outrage.

These meanings of the two related words obviously don't fit
together. Which is the reason why, since 1792, people have
mixed them up and have used *enormity* more and more often
to mean vast size.

When the *Oxford English Dictionary,* sometime around 1890, got to *enormity,* it marked this secondary meaning as obsolete and added, "Recent examples might perhaps be found, but the use is now regarded as incorrect."

Well, the doctrine of correctness in grammar and usage has long since bit the dust and is now considered nonsensical by professional linguists. Millions of people since 1890 have used *enormity* to mean vast size in speaking and writing. For instance, in an article on the division of Palestine in 1947 (*New York Times Magazine,* 11/21/82) the author writes: "The Zionist lobbyists . . . contemplated the enormity of the effort that lay ahead."

All major dictionaries duly list the secondary meaning of *enormity* as "enormous size." Nevertheless, the purists simply don't admit defeat. In the *Harper Dictionary of Contemporary Usage* (1975) the authors, William and Mary Morris, asked the members of their usage panel whether they agreed with the use of the word *enormity* to mean vast size. The panel consisted of 136 writers and journalists, most of them conservative and elderly.

Only 31 percent of the panel members approved the use of *enormity* to mean vast size; 69 percent disagreed, some of them violently.

Hal Borland said, "God no!"

John Brooks said, "Gawd!"

Elizabeth Janeway said, "No, I regard this usage as an enormity."

Orville Prescott said, "Vile, ignorant usage."

F. D. Reeve said, "No, Wow!"

Rex Stout said, "No, No, No, No."

The whole thing is strange. Trivial differences in usage get respectable elderly writers foaming at the mouth. What does it matter? Why do they get so excited?

I call it the "correct usage neurosis."

feisty. *Feisty* is a common, even fashionable slang word. The unabridged *Random House Dictionary* says it comes from *feist,* "a small mongrel dog, esp. one that is ill-tempered; cur; mutt (short for *feisting* cur, from Middle English, Old English *feisting,* breaking wind)."

From these unappetizing origins *feisty* has come to mean fidgety, touchy, quarrelsome, quick-tempered, scrappy, frisky and exuberant, lively, energetic, full of spirit.

As time went by and the word was used more and more often, its connotations gradually changed and from being almost an insult it became downright complimentary.

In the fall of 1982 there was a race for the U.S. Senate in New Jersey between a somewhat dull middle-aged businessman, Frank Lautenberg, and a 72-year-old longtime Congresswoman, Millicent Fenwick. She had gained national fame as a maverick, an independent spirit, an original, and a pipe-smoking grandmother. She spoke her mind freely and charmed everyone. Eventually she lost to Mr. Lautenberg by a very close vote.

A few days before the election, the inevitable happened. Lautenberg (*New York Times,* 10/28/82) called the aristocratic old lady "feisty."

fishy. The other day (12/9/82) William Safire wrote in his political *New York Times* column about Richard Wirthlin, President Reagan's pollster. Wirthlin's firm, he wrote, did a survey for the Institute of Arab Studies. "Most people," Safire said, "think this looks fishy."

Everybody knows what *fishy* means. It's slang—or at least "informal"—but it's one of the most widely used and indispensable words in the English language.

I looked through all my dictionaries and found a great variety of definitions: of dubious quality, unreliable, questionable, shady, improbable, causing doubt or suspicion, odd, unlikely, doubtful, causing disbelief, suggestive of deception, dishonest, unethical, insincere, untruthful, unconvincing, unbelievable, not quite right or true.

Eighteen different definitions and not a single one that says *exactly* what *fishy* means! Why? Because the word, with its unique blend of smelliness and slipperiness, simply can't be replaced by another. Disraeli used it in 1844 in his novel *Coningsby* and it has been used millions of times since.

It's one of the great treasures of the English language.

flab.   *Webster's New World Dictionary,* which tends to rather brutal definitions sometimes, defines *flab* as "sagging, flaccid flesh." It says the word is a back-formation from *flabby* and labels it "Colloq."

Other dictionaries are more indulgent toward this unhappy word. *Webster's Collegiate* says "soft flabby body tissue" and the *Oxford American Dictionary* simply says "fat, flabbiness." *Random House* skips the word altogether, either because of an oversight or to spare the dictionary users' feelings.

Neither *Webster's Collegiate* nor *American Heritage* considers the word slang or in any way objectionable. Unpleasant, yes; but fully respectable as an English word.

Flab started as a schoolboy joke. The *Supplement to the Oxford English Dictionary* quotes a 1959 book by I. and E. Opie, *Lore and Language of Schoolchildren:* "The unfortunate fat boy is known as flab."

Nowadays *flab* is a universal phenomenon and a common word. *Newsweek* (11/22/82) wrote, "American adults are sweating themselves into shape as never before, but the nation's youngsters are going to flab."

An ugly word, but ours. It has found its niche in the nation's vocabulary.

flak.   When three new shelters for the homeless were opened in New York City, the *New York Times* (1/22/83) wrote, "Mayor Koch will have to bear the main political flak from residents near those buildings who will likely complain about having down-and-outers in their neighborhoods."

What is *flak?* It's easier to understand what the word means if you know where it comes from. During World War II the Germans developed special antiaircraft guns, which they called *Fliegerabwehrkanonen.* The German acronym for that was *flak.* So when the Allied planes flew over German-occupied territory, they exposed themselves to flak from the ground.

Some fifteen years ago, *flak* began to be used in the figurative sense. As soon as a political move was made, those affected started their flak—that is, a lot of ack-ack-ack noise attacking the move.

Flak is something you raise or take. It's part of the political game. There's lobbying by the pros and flak by the antis.

flaky.   First there was the word *screwball*. It came from baseball and meant, as you would expect, "a ball pitched with reverse spin against the natural curve."

In the 1920s those who could perform this feat were called screwballs themselves and the word was normally used with loving admiration. A little while later, the word *screwball* began to be used outside of baseball and meant generally a whimsically eccentric person with unusual ideas. It wasn't a word of contempt; rather, it was used with a smile.

Fashions in words change, and after thirty or forty years of saying *screwball* people got tired of the word and replaced it with *flake* and *flaky*. The meaning is still exactly the same—a *flake* is just as unpredictable as a snowflake, or as a screwball, for that matter.

Flaky means eccentric, but not crazy. We have lots of words that mean crazy in various degrees, but we have few words that mean exactly what is implied by calling someone flaky. Again, *flaky* is spoken or written with mild approval and more or less secret admiration for someone who flouts the rules of socially approved behavior. We love individualists.

But that doesn't mean we're eager to live with them. *Time* (1/10/83) ran a piece about classified love ads. Do the respondents to those ads have any complaints? Yes. "The most frequent complaint from men is that the women weigh more than they say. The women complain that the men are flaky."

flap.   In the fall of 1982 poor, unemployed people from all over the country came to Houston, Texas, and set up a tent city thirty miles from downtown. They were soon discovered by the media. Reporters and TV crews appeared, everybody was photographed and interviewed again and again. There was a circus atmosphere and the Houston tent city became a national phenomenon. The whole thing turned into a gigantic publicity stunt.

When the *Wall Street Journal* reported the story (1/14/83) the copyreader put the following headline on it:

Houston's Tent City Gets Into a
Big Flap Over Publicity Blitz

This, of course, is a pun. In my opinion it's quite a good one. *Flap* means the loose-hanging side of a tent or, as a slang word, a commotion. So readers of the *Wall Street Journal* got a bit of extra amusement for their money.

Lots of people are prejudiced against puns, but not today's journalists. They use puns whenever they can. For all I know, they're now trained in punning and learn how to do it in journalism school.

I like puns and am enjoying the many, many puns I now get gratis with my papers and magazines. Puns are fun to read.

H. W. Fowler, the crusty old author of *Modern English Usage,* wrote one of his inimitable brief paragraphs about puns:

> *The assumption that puns are* per se *contemptible, betrayed by the habit of describing every pun not as* a pun, *but as* a bad pun *or* a feeble pun, *is a sign at once of sheepish docility and desire to seem superior. Puns are good, bad, and indifferent, and only those who lack the wit to make them are unaware of the fact.*

flipflop.   A flipflop is a backward handspring or somersault. *Webster's New World Dictionary* explains in more detail: "an acrobatic spring backward from the feet to the hands and back to the feet."

Flipflops (first spelled *flipflaps*) have appeared in print since the 17th century. They must have been known and performed since time immemorial.

When was *flipflop* first used as a metaphor for sudden changes in attitude or policy? As, for instance, in William Safire's column in the *New York Times* (2/21/83)? Safire wrote about President Reagan's promise, in his election campaign, to push for an undivided Jerusalem under Israeli sovereignty. Two years later, Reagan said this was a matter of negotiation between the Israelis and the Arabs. Safire called this "the Reagan flipflop."

The metaphorical use of the word *flipflop* is only about thirty years old. Before that, a sudden change from one policy to another was called an about-face or a turnaround. When these terms wore out, someone thought of a flipflop—a strenuous and highly skilled acrobatic feat, impossible for an ordinary person to perform. Nothing could be more vivid to describe an act of betrayal.

Now, thirty years later, *flipflop* is just a word like any other. You read about a flipflop and understand that some politician has turned around. No picture of a backward handspring arises in your mind.

Soon we'll have to think of something a little more vivid.

floozie.   There are few words in the English language that are defined in totally different terms in different dictionaries.

If you look up *floozie* in *Webster's Collegiate,* you'll find that the word means "a tawdry or immoral woman, *specif:* prostitute."

But if you look up *floozie* in the *Dictionary of American Slang* by Wentworth and Flexner, you'll find the following tender statement: "A girl; an average girl or young woman with a good but not beautiful face, an open, honest personality, and a good spirit, but lacking in deep insight, good taste, refinement, and with no more and probably less than average intelligence."

It's true that this is only the first of two lengthy definitions given by Wentworth and Flexner, but the second one, though somewhat harsher than the first, goes only as far as calling a floozie "a cheap or loose girl or woman."

Wentworth and Flexner clearly have a soft spot for floozies. For them, there is a world of difference between a floozie and a prostitute. Why, if every floozie was a prostitute, we wouldn't need the fluffy, soft, gentle word *floozie* to describe a certain type of girl or woman.

Frank Rich, the theater critic of the *New York Times,* recently (12/22/82) wrote about an actress: "She gives us a light-weight floozie, not a predatory animal."

Obviously, when it comes to floozies, he's a Wentworth and Flexner man.

flunk.   The other day I read about someone who "flunked a lie detector test" (*Nation,* 11/13/82).

This started me thinking. What if the reporter had written, "He failed a lie detector test"? Surely that wouldn't have meant the same thing at all. If someone failed a lie detector test, that's a simple statement of fact. He may have failed the test for all kinds of reasons, some of them quite innocent. But if you say that he *flunked* the test, the clear implication is that he's a liar.

Why is this so? Because the word *flunk,* first found in print in 1823, is a blend of the words *flinch* and *funk.* To *flinch* means to draw back or shrink away; to *funk* means to be afraid. So *flunk,* even if you don't know about its derivation, carries with it a feeling of moral guilt. You flunked the exam because you didn't work hard enough. Flunking is your own fault but failure may have been an act of God.

Besides, flunking means more than just failing. If the passing grade was 65 and you made only 64, you failed. But if you made 25, you *flunked.*

fly. On January 8, 1983, the *New York Times* TV critic Walter Goodman wrote about a TV pilot, a show that had been rejected by NBC: "One assumes that at some stage in the production of this show, NBC's market researchers discovered that a little Puerto Rican cop, no matter how likable, just wouldn't fly."

The word *fly*, as used here, is clearly slang. In fact, it is such a recent slang word that I had to hunt through most dictionaries until I finally found it in the 1975 second supplement to Wentworth and Flexner's *Dictionary of American Slang.* There it was: the third meaning listed for the verb *fly*, with a quote dated 1973: "Nixon's speech didn't fly." The definition read: "To be convincing; go over."

Now the point is this. The *New York Times Manual of Style and Usage* (2d ed. 1976) says: "*Slang and colloquialisms.* Use only in appropriate contexts." So what should Goodman have done when the word *fly* came to his mind? Replace it instantly with *go over?* Or stop writing until he figured out whether his TV review was an appropriate context for *fly?* Or consult with one or more of his colleagues? Or look up *fly*, meaning "go over" in the dictionary? The *Times* style manual recommends *Webster's New World* and, if a word isn't listed there, the unabridged *Webster's Third.* As I said, *fly* in the sense of "go over" isn't listed in either.

Of course, this whole thing is ridiculous. *Fly* is now a perfectly good word, known to all readers of the *Times* in the sense Goodman was using it.

Besides, *fly*, as used here, doesn't mean exactly "be convincing" or "go over." It means "get good ratings for thirteen weeks and then be renewed." Isn't it simpler to say *fly?*

footsie. In her review of the movie *The Verdict*, Pauline Kael of *The New Yorker* (1/10/83) described the courtroom scene, "The judge is grossly prejudiced—he plays footsie with the Church."

What does *playing footsie* mean? It means—or meant—exactly what you think. Wentworth and Flexner's *Dictionary of American Slang,* which goes in for detailed definitions, says: "The pedal equivalent of amorous hand-holding; touching, pushing and/or more or less clumsily caressing with one's foot, as under a table, a foot or the feet of one of the opposite sex."

A quote, dated 1944, shows this literal meaning of the phrase. Gene Fowler, in his book *Good Night, Sweet Prince,* wrote "I played footsie with her during Don José's first seduction by Carmen."

After the 1940s the phrase *playing footsie* fell into a decline. Instead of referring to a pleasant game of sexual dalliance, it began to be used almost exclusively in a totally nonsexual sense. *Playing footsie* now usually means surreptitious, underhanded dealings with the police, the government, corporations or, as in the example I quoted, the Catholic Church.

In 1963 *The Economist* wrote, "Pakistan is . . . despite recent games of footsie with Peking, a staunchly anti-communist ally."

The Pakistan-Peking type of footsie-playing can't be much fun.

for free.   A true-blue purist will treat the expression *for free* with utter contempt. "Slang," write William and Mary Morris in the *Harper Dictionary of Contemporary Usage* (1975), "used only facetiously by careful writers." "Semi-humorous slang," says Theodore Bernstein in *The Careful Writer* (1965), "perhaps originally used by semiliterates."

On the other hand, to scientific linguists, *for free* is just another idiom. The *Supplement to the Oxford English Dictionary* (1972) calmly notes under *for:* "With an adjective, in pleonastic use as *for free,* for no charge, without payment," and follows this with half a dozen quotations from reputable literary sources.

Today, *for free* is quite common. An article on international trade in the *New Republic* (11/15/82) says that if the Japanese don't buy goods from us for American dollars, "we've got the Sonys and Toyotas for free."

Of course, to say *for free* when you mean "for nothing" doesn't make sense. But the English language is full of idioms that don't make sense, if you analyze them with a microscope and see if they stand up logically. We say "I don't hardly know" and "I couldn't help laughing" and lots of other idioms of that sort.

Let's just accept the fact that the English language is full of oddities and quirks.

That's what makes it so charming.

fulsome.   In the fall of 1982 Peter Prescott of *Newsweek* started a book review with the words, "A writer whose first novel is fulsomely praised must pay forever after an excruciating tax."

This brought a letter from a reader pointing out the "erroneous use of the word *fulsome.*"

He was answered by Priscilla Baker of *Newsweek:* "*Fulsome,* according to the first definition in *Webster's Third International Dictionary,* [means] copious, abundant." Prescott had been right.

In the *New York Times* (1/2/83), William Safire jumped into the fray. "The permissiveness of the *Merriam-Webster Third* is legendary," he wrote. "To most lexicographers and to most careful users of the language, the word *fulsome* means 'disgusting, offensive because excessive and insincere.'"

Safire was only half right. It's true that all major dictionaries except the *Merriam-Webster* ones (*Webster's Third* and *Webster's Collegiate*) define *fulsome* as "disgusting and offensive." But Merriam-Webster is backed by the latest research. Here's the story.

From 1250 on, *fulsome* was used to mean "copious and abundant." Then in 1663 a new meaning took over: "offensive because of gross and excessive flattery." But around 1968 the meaning shifted again back to "copious and abundant." There are plenty of quotes for this old-new usage in the *Second Barnhart Dictionary of New English* (1980).

So *Newsweek* wins, Safire loses.

If you want to use *fulsome* in the sense of copious and abundant, go right ahead.

fun.   On February 7, 1983, *Newsweek* ran a cover story on brain research. It quoted Dr. Michael Brownstein, a researcher at the National Institute of Mental Health: "This is a fun time to be doing neuroscience. A lot of good people see it as the last frontier."

The use of the word *fun* as an adjective is only about twenty years old. It's the kind of thing that drives purists up the wall.

I looked up the adjective *fun* in the four major desk dictionaries.

Webster's Collegiate lists it without comment, defines it as "providing entertainment, amusement, or enjoyment," and gives two examples, "a fun party" and "a fun person to be with."

Random House College says it's informal and defines it as "of or pertaining to fun, esp. to social fun." No examples.

Webster's New World says it's colloquial and defines it as "intended for, or giving, pleasure and amusement." Example: "a fun gift."

American Heritage, published in 1982, simply ignores *fun* as an adjective. So does the other recent purist dictionary, the *Oxford American Dictionary* (1980).

Apparently those two diehards think if you just ignore a usage you don't like, it'll go away.

I don't think it will.

funky.   The *New York Times* (12/22/82) reviewed a jazz concert in the White House: "While the audience dressed with impeccable etiquette, Dizzy Gillespie, in a patterned sports shirt, didn't even bother to wear a tie, and Chick Corea managed to retain his funky casual look."

The *Times* was using *funky* in its traditional sense. The *Supplement to the Oxford English Dictionary* says, "down-to-earth and uncomplicated; emotional; having the qualities of the blues." It's a quality that reminds us of the early days of jazz. There's a bittersweet, sad feeling, an atmosphere of slow-paced melancholy.

At least, that's what *funky* used to mean ever since the 1950s. But many years have passed since then, and *funky* has become high fashion. Now it also means simply swinging or in. Reviewing a recent novel, the *New York Review of Books* says (6/10/82): "Steeped in a cultured funk, [John Hawkes's] novels strive to be erotically rich and dark and Continental— pillowbooks for postmodernists." Try to figure out for yourself what *funk* means in this sentence.

It's too bad. *Funky* still means something that has to do with the original sound of the blues. Maybe in a few years that nostalgic meaning will be gone forever.

gaga. *Gaga* is a slang word meaning crazy, foolish, marked by wild enthusiasm, infatuated.

A Goo Goo Cluster, on the other hand, is a kind of candy manufactured in Nashville, Tennessee. It was the subject of one of those amusing front-page articles that appear almost daily in the *Wall Street Journal* (12/8/82).

The article described Goo Goos as a mixture of chocolate, peanuts, caramel and marshmallows. They're made by the Standard Candy Company of Nashville. For many years they've been a favorite of Tennesseans, but lately the company decided to branch out and invade the North. Since the fall of 1982, Goo Goo Clusters, at $10 for a box of twenty-four, have been stocked by Bloomingdale's in New York City, and the palates of Northerners seem to welcome them.

The article went to great length analyzing the astounding success and mysterious appeal of Goo Goos. Down the middle of the page the copyreader felt the need for inserting a subhead. What was it? You guessed it:

Gaga Over Goo Goos

gas. *Gas* is probably one of the most common words in the American language. And 999 times out of a thousand it's used as a shortened form of *gasoline;* the thousandth time it means any kind of airlike fluid that isn't air.

The word *gas* in the sense of an airlike fluid was invented by the Dutch chemist J. B. van Helmont (1577–1644) on the model of the Greek word *chaos.* The word *gas* in the sense of gasoline was invented by the American people almost at the same time as the automobile. It appeared in print for the first time in 1905. Dictionaries list this meaning of gas with the label *"U.S. Informal."*

So far so good. But the *New York Times,* probably ever since 1905, has had tremendous trouble squeezing the long word *gasoline* into a headline. Its solution, for three-quarters of a century, has been to use the "proper" word *gasoline* in the text and the abbreviation *gas* in the headline, but always with chaste quotation marks around it. Obviously the device was meant to show that the *Times* ordinarily wouldn't touch such a vulgar word with a ten-foot pole, but occasionally had to yield to necessity in a headline. The quotation marks were meant to apologize for possibly hurting the tender feelings of a well-brought-up matron in Scarsdale whose sheltered life might be unduly disturbed by such uncouth language.

But the world moves on. On November 10, 1982, the *Times* front page carried the headline

Gas Tax Rise Urged by Rostenkowski for Road Repairs

The word *gas* was quite indecently naked—no quotation marks. To be sure, *gas* never appeared in the article itself, although *gasoline* was mentioned six times.

Progress is slow but sure. By the year 2000, *gas* (for *gasoline*) may sneak its way into the text of the *New York Times.*

gay. On November 11, 1982, I discovered that the *New York Times* is apparently the last holdout in the country against the use of the word *gay* in the sense of homosexual.

The *New York Times Manual of Style and Usage* (1976) says, "*gay.* Do not use as a synonym for *homosexual* unless it appears in the formal capitalized name of an organization or in quoted matter."

Following this rule, the article was called "Death Benefit Voted for Homosexual Lover." It told about a San Francisco homosexual who was awarded survivor's death benefits after the death of the man he lived with. The article used the word *homosexual* six times and the word *gay* only once, in a quoted statement from the beneficiary, Mr. Smith. He said, "The settlement sets a moral precedent in showing that gay relationships can stand alongside straight relationships as equal."

The first printed use of *gay* in the sense of *homosexual* dates back to 1935. By now, after forty-eight years, the usage is universal. It is listed as slang in *Webster's New World Dictionary* and the *Random House Dictionary,* and without any usage label in *Webster's Collegiate, American Heritage* (2d ed.), and the *New York Times'* own *Everyday Dictionary* (1982). In other words, the word is now fully accepted and there's no reason why you shouldn't use it in speaking or writing.

Never mind the *New York Times.*

gee-whiz.   First, there's the word *gee,* as in the head-line *"Gee! The G24—A Sports Car for Chrysler"* (*Time,* 1/17/83).

Gee is an exclamation of surprise, wonder, enthusiasm, or just mild emphasis. It's a short form of the exclamation *Jesus!* The *Supplement to the Oxford English Dictionary* has traced *gee* back to Stephen Crane's *The Red Badge of Courage* (1895), which contains the sentence "Gee rod! how we will thump 'em!"

Second, there's the word *whiz,* as in "Tip O'Neill is being knocked for not being a whiz on substance" (*New Republic,* 1/24/83). A *whiz* is a top expert, and the adjective *whiz* or *whiz-bang* means first-rate or topnotch. *Whiz* has to do with *wizard* and has been used since at least 1920, when F. Scott Fitzgerald wrote in *This Side of Paradise:* "Wonderful night. 'It's a whiz.'"

Third, there's the combination *gee whiz,* which means the same as *gee!* only more so. It's been traced back to the 1880s. In 1922, Sinclair Lewis wrote in *Babbitt:* "Awful good to get back to civilization! Gee whiz, those Main Street burgs are slow." In 1957, J. D. Salinger wrote in *Franny and Zooey:* "Well, gee whiz, I'm only trying to make polite bathroom talk."

Fourth and finally, there's *gee-whiz,* as in the example I recently found in *Newsweek* (2/14/83): "Verging on editorial overkill, the March issue of *Motor Trend* magazine devotes no fewer than 39 gee-whiz pages to the new Corvette."

So *gee-whiz* has come full circle. First there was *gee,* an exclamation of awe. Then there was *gee whiz,* the same with double strength. Then *gee whiz* deteriorated to an expression of mild, almost inaudible emphasis. And finally it has come to mean nothing but mockery and irony. *Gee-whiz* now means silly, overblown hype, faked enthusiasm, ridiculous artificial excitement.

get a fix. On November 16, 1982, a few days after Yuri Andropov succeeded Leonid Brezhnev as the leader of the Soviet Union, the *New York Times* ran an article with the headline

Hard to "Get Fix" on Soviet Leader

I was puzzled by the quotation marks around *get fix.* Was this a taboo expression around the editorial offices of the *Times?* Considering the fact that it is a perfectly ordinary English phrase, this seemed hard to believe.

Why then? I studied the article to find out. It dealt with the difficulties of getting a clear picture of Andropov and relied in part on a Sunday TV interview with Malcolm Toon, the U.S. Ambassador to Moscow from 1976 to 1979.

Mr. Toon had said, in front of millions of viewers, that he "was not able to get a fix on the man." He also said, "I frankly don't know whether the guy speaks English or not."

From this I deduced that the *Times* headline writer used the phrase *get fix* because he rightly shied away from writing

Almost Nothing Known About Andropov

Yet the phrase *get a fix* made the headline writer uneasy. *Fix* is one of those wonderful all-purpose words that are the glory of the English language. The *Random House College Dictionary* (rev. ed.) lists thirty-one different meanings of *fix*. Five of them are labeled "Informal" (fix a jury, get even with, spay a pet, predicament, etc.); two are labeled "Slang" (injection of heroin, underhanded arrangement).

Get a fix, as used by Ambassador Toon, is one of the twenty-four perfectly straightforward and formal uses of the word *fix*. It is a nautical term referring to "the charted position of a vessel or aircraft determined by two or more bearings taken by landmarks, heavenly bodies, etc." The ambassador used the word figuratively and quite elegantly.

But the *Times* headline writer didn't take any chances. *Any* use of the word *fix*, in the eyes of the *Times*, is suspect. Let's put quotes around the word and play it safe.

You can't rely on ex-ambassadors to use language fit for the readers of the *New York Times.*

gimmick.   What exactly is a *gimmick?* It's a word that's hard to define, but easy to illustrate. On November 1, 1982, the *New York Times* wrote, "The Republican Party, never slow to pick up on a popular fund-raising gimmick, has issued its

first mail order gift catalogue, just in time for Christmas."
Three weeks later (11/19/82) the paper wrote, "Straining for a
new gimmick in the old police-drama formula . . . tomorrow's
television movie . . . comes up with a deaf cop." Three days
later (11/22/82) *Newsweek* wrote, "A thriller in which a psychiatrist solves the murder by interpreting a dream? There
hasn't been such a dime-store Freudian gimmick since the
days when there were dime stores."

As these three examples show, a gimmick is a piece of
trickery. The inventor contrives some business—not necessarily fraudulent but highly ingenious—that will attract
suckers. Normally, people don't vote for political parties to
get a gift, deaf cops don't catch criminals, and murders aren't
solved by interpreting dreams.

The word *gimmick* is said to come from the word *gimac,* an
anagram of *magic* used among professional magicians to talk
about their trade secrets. Well, as everyone knows, magicians
don't use real magic, but tricks.

The word *gimmick* is always used with contempt. If you call
something a gimmick, you warn people not to fall for it.

But then, just as people enjoy watching magicians even
though they know it's all a bunch of tricks, so they like a
gimmick.

Without gimmicks, the world would be a much duller
place.

gizmo. In reviewing a new book for investors, the *Wall
Street Journal* (10/26/82) writes, "No fancy financial gizmos
here, not even a 12-button calculator."

What is a *gizmo* (or *gismo*)? It's something you don't know
the name of—a gadget, a gimmick, a thing.

And where does the strange word *gizmo* come from? *Web-*

ster's Collegiate and *American Heritage* are in full agreement on that point. They say the word is of unknown origin. *Random House* simply says, "?"

Webster's New World, as usual, goes into all kinds of speculation. I quote verbatim: "? Sp. *gisma*, obs. or dial. var. of *chisme*, trifle, jigger, ult. L. *cimex*, a bug." Nice work!

Gizmo, whatever its origin, is one of those many, many words the English language has in reserve if you can't think of the proper word for something. *The Synonym Finder* by J. M. Rodale (1978) offers this choice: "gadget, mickey, widget, contraption, whachamacallit, thingumajig, thingamabob, doohickey, do-hinkey, dingus, doodad, gismo, fandangle."

I knew all of those, except *fandangle,* which is listed in the unabridged *Webster's Third,* but with the meaning of "nonsense." Then there is my private favorite, "doojeehunkus," which is listed absolutely nowhere. (I guess I made it up.)

What a glorious language English is! It not only has vast numbers of words for everything under the sun, it also has a glittering array of words for things you can't name.

glitch.   Back in 1970, *Science News* carried the following elaborate explanation: "It appeared that for two pulsars at least the gradual slowdown was occasionally punctuated by jerks, sudden speedups, after which the slowdown resumed. These were called sudden events, or glitches, a word borrowed from the jargon of the astronauts."

And where did the astronauts get the word *glitch?* Apparently from their German tutors, like Wernher von Braun. (*Glitschig,* in German, means slippery.)

So, from outer space, *glitch* got into the language. Naturally, as the word became more widely known, it lost its technical and scientific connotations and became just a general word for mishap, slipup, boo-boo.

By now it's used quite indiscriminately. A recent (1/4/83) headline in the *New York Times* read: "Publishers Battle the Goof and the Glitch."

What were those goofs and glitches?

One was that the jacket of Bernard Malamud's novel *God's Grace* identified him as the author of *The Centaur. The Centaur* was written by John Updike.

Another one was the opening sentence in Beverly Sills's autobiography: "When I was only three, and still named Belle Miriam Silverman, I sang my first aria in pubic."

glitzy.   In the fall of 1982 the newspapers and magazines were full of stories about John Z. DeLorean, an automobile manufacturer who had been arrested on cocaine conspiracy charges. *Time* (11/1/82) wrote about him: "He had charmed his way into the glitzy show-biz celebrity circles, dating the likes of Candice Bergen, Nancy Sinatra and Ursula Andress."

Glitzy means just what it sounds like. It means glittery, showy, spectacular, flashy. The word was first spotted in print in 1968. It seems to be derived, through Yiddish, from the German word *glitzern,* which means to glitter. I also suspect that it echoes the word *ritzy,* which was derived from César Ritz, the 19th-century founder of the famous Ritz luxury hotels. *Ritzy* means luxurious, fashionable, elegant.

There's an ever-changing fashion in the words we use to mean fashionable. Think of *swank, posh, classy*—the words come and go. They all seem to start with genuine admiration of wealth and elegance and end up with a growing feeling of irony and envy.

Now the in word is *glitzy.* I have in my collection newspaper and magazine references to glitzy movies (*Nation,* 1/1/83), glitzy restaurants (*Wall Street Journal,* 12/6/82), and even glitzy graphics in TV news broadcasts (*Newsweek,* 11/15/82).

Sooner or later we'll get tired of *glitzy* and switch to a new word. I wonder what it'll be.

Subdued, perhaps?

gofer.   *Time* (11/1/82) had a long story on the DeLorean cocaine deal. It said the car with the cocaine was driven by a gofer to the airport.

What is a *gofer?* The word has an interesting history.

A gopher (with *ph)* is a little scurrying ratlike animal. Around 1950 or so, someone in the theater thought of a little pun and coined the word *gopher* for a stagestruck, unpaid hanger-on who was gladly at the beck and call of everyone to "go for" coffee or cigarettes.

So *gopher* became the word for the person at the bottom of the totem pole who had to run errands for everyone else.

Time passed. The pun stopped being funny. The spelling of the word changed from *gopher* to *gofer.* In the 1975 supplement to Wentworth and Flexner's *Dictionary of American Slang* a *gofer* is now formally defined as "an employee in an office, construction site, etc., part of whose duties are to run errands for other employees."

Pretty soon there'll be an official gofers' union, they'll get minimum wages, and there'll be a job description that spells out what beverages and other items they're supposed to fetch and carry. The name *gofer* will be changed to "Assistant for Outside Procurement."

I'm all for that. Much better than exploiting people's enthusiasm.

goodies.   *Goodies,* of course, is a word used mainly with and by children. It means, first of all, sweets, and then, by extension, all kinds of things children like.

It's always labeled as an informal word, which doesn't present too many problems as long as we are dealing with goodies for children. But *goodies* is also used to mean delightful and attractive things for grownups, and the purists don't like that.

Every year, for instance, around income tax legislation time, Congress or the Administration comes up with a lot of goodies—loopholes and such—that give delight to scores of lobbyists and special interest groups. Tax bills traditionally are "hung with goodies like a Christmas tree."

In a recent book review in the *New Republic* (12/6/82), the reviewer discussed a new book of short stories by Evelyn Waugh. He wrote about "Waugh's stabs at his lifelong theme, in which the worthy junior is shafted by the convention that seniors, no matter how undeserving, get the goodies."

Goodies, in this instance, means a toy auto presented by an uncle, a higher rank in an English public school, a large share of an inheritance, and much, much more.

As you see, the word *goodies* can have a very serious meaning.

goofy.   In a story about the actor Paul Newman, *Newsweek* (12/6/82) tells about a waitress who is staring at Newman in a restaurant. "He twists his nose goofily between thumb and forefinger and goes cross-eyed; she turns pinker and hides her face, bubbling with giggles."

This little scene shows graphically the present meaning and feeling of the word *goofy.* It's silly, childish, ridiculous behavior. If you say someone behaves goofily, it's a comical interlude, possibly intended as a joke. It doesn't mean the person is congenitally stupid or foolish. It's not an insult.

In the 1920s, the word *goof* meant something far more serious. Wentworth and Flexner, in their *Dictionary of American Slang,* say that "unlike a sap, dope, boob, or jerk, a goof was tragically stupid on all subjects at all times, and his stupidity was not due to lack of experience or innocence and was never funny." After World War II, that meaning faded away. The word *goof* was used for a mistake or blunder or for *making* a mistake or blunder.

Goofy, like many other slang words, has become soft and even affectionate. *Random House* defines *goofy* as "ridiculous; silly; wacky; nutty" and gives the example "a goofy little hat."

gosh.   Whenever anything newsworthy happens, the reporter assigned to the story will phone around and collect comments from people in the know. So, when President Reagan named W. Paul Thayer as Deputy Secretary of Defense, the *New York Times* (12/7/82) printed a verbatim comment from Charls Walker, a Washington lobbyist.

"Gosh," Walker said, "he knows the industry backwards and forwards."

In this way, the word *gosh* made its appearance in the *Times*—possibly for the first time.

You'll say that doesn't count. It wasn't the *Times* that used that slang word, it was Mr. Walker.

But wait a minute. Since all reporters now routinely quote informants verbatim—which they didn't do twenty or thirty years ago—it really comes to the same thing. The *Times* is now full of exact quotes of what people *said,* and naturally that makes for a high percentage of slang. A generation ago, the reporter would have ignored the word *gosh* and quoted Mr. Walker as simply saying, "He knows the industry backwards and forwards." Now he hears Walker say "Gosh," so he includes it in his copy.

It makes an enormous difference.

In the first place, adding "gosh" makes the quoted pronouncement sound more authentic. If Mr. Walker is quoted as saying "gosh," you get the feeling you know he really said whatever he said.

Second, the word *gosh* makes Walker's comment more convincing. Clearly, he's a man who knows what he's talking about and is emphatic in saying so.

And third, it makes the whole article more pleasant to read. It's nicer with the "gosh" included.

During the past ten or twenty years, the *Times* has added innumerable special departments and features, all aimed at entertaining its readers. Among a thousand other things, it has also added a vast amount of informal and slangy words. For my 30 cents I now get not only all the stiff, formal words I used to get in the past, I also get *kids* and *nuts* and *cops* and *gosh*.

It's a daily pleasure.

grandma.   In his column summarizing the events of 1982, George Will wrote (*Newsweek,* 1/3/83): "Britain's youngest prince has a grandma unruffled by commoners who drop by to chat in her bedroom in the wee small hours."

Will is a fine writer who knows how to make his columns more pleasant to read by the occasional informal word. What could be more informal and, literally, more familiar than *grandma?* The readers of *Newsweek* will like it much better than "the Queen" (with a capital Q) or "Her Majesty." It'll give them a nice feeling of being on smiling terms with Elizabeth II.

Of course, this is America and it took us a revolution to be able to write in such a way about kings and queens. Would a

British journalist have the same freedom? I'm not sure. The *Random House Dictionary* defines *lese majesty* as "*Law*. a crime or offense against the sovereign power in a state, esp. against the dignity of a ruler."

Maybe the British royal family has mellowed. One thing is sure: Queen Victoria would have been furious if one of her subjects had dared to call her "grandma."

There are many, many reasons why I prefer to live now than at any other period of history. The use of *grandma* in referring to the queen of England is one of them.

groupie   Until the late 1960s there weren't any groupies and therefore there was no word for the phenomenon. Then they appeared in great swarms and a word had to be found to describe them. Wentworth and Flexner's *Dictionary of American Slang* has the classic definition: "A girl who seeks out, or follows on tour, star entertainers, esp. members of rock groups or pop singers, in order to gain prestige through sexual favors."

The word immediately became something of a technical term, but it took the *New York Times* a dozen years or so to mention groupies. On October 31, 1982, in an article on the use of cocaine in Hollywood, the paper referred to Cathy Evelyn Smith, who was with the actor John Belushi when he died. "Miss Smith," said the paper, "who investigators have said was a former rock music groupie . . ." A few weeks later, on December 7, 1982, there was a piece about video games. "Data Age," it said, "has produced a rock music video game cartridge. . . . (The challenge: get the band members through a crowd of crazed groupies to a waiting limousine.)"

Groupies are now simply a feature of American life. But the word has had further adventures. As soon as it became widely known, it began to be used figuratively for *any* ardent fan of *anything*. George Will, the *Newsweek* columnist, started a column (3/1/82) this way: "Ramsey Clark, that groupie of anti-American dictators . . . "

No more wild screams, no more ear-splitting music, no sex—just a word that's a little sharper than *fan*.

gumption.   James Reston, the senior political columnist of the *New York Times*, said in his column (10/20/82): "The Israelis and the Arabs . . . seem to agree that Uncle Sam could solve their problems if only he had enough gumption to follow their contradictory advice."

Gumption is a fascinating word. No one is quite sure where it comes from. Most dictionaries say it derives from Scottish dialect, and has something to do with the Middle English word *gome*, which meant attention. Somewhere along the way it acquired the joky Latin ending -*tion*, which accounts for the fact that most dictionaries consider it "colloquial" and don't accept it as a serious English word.

It first showed up in print in 1719 and for the first hundred years or so simply meant common sense, shrewdness in practical affairs. Then slowly the meaning changed. In 1825 there was a dictionary entry that said, "Common sense, combined with energy." Gradually the main meaning became "initiative, enterprise, drive" until by now *gumption* stands mainly for courage and boldness.

In the latest edition of the *Random House Dictionary*, the definition reads: "*Informal*. Initiative, aggressiveness, resourcefulness, courage, spunk, guts."

What a word! Its history teaches us that plain old common sense is the foundation of courage and enterprise.

guru.   Back in the early 17th century, British travelers to India brought back news about holy men, teaching priests who kept little schools where they instructed their followers in the secrets of the universe. They were called *gooroos,* which was a Sanskrit word meaning grave, dignified, weighty.

Indian gooroos—or *gurus,* as they're now spelled—are still around. You think of them as Gandhi-like figures, sitting cross-legged, wearing nothing but a loincloth, and occasionally dropping pearls of wisdom to their disciples.

Suddenly, in the mid-'60s, the word *guru* became fashionable in the United States. *Guru* became the word for *any* kind of teacher of adult groups. There were sports gurus, Wall Street gurus, ladies' fashions gurus, income tax gurus—whathave-you. A guru was just a wise man, with nothing religious about him.

On February 28, 1983, *Newsweek* carried the headline

The Democrats' New Guru

The piece dealt with Professor Robert B. Reich, a 36-year-old Harvard economist, who furnished ideas to Democratic presidential aspirants. He proposed to save ailing industries by specialty orders and high technology, he was for replacing the income tax with a consumption tax, he'd give workers vouchers for retraining.

There was a picture of Reich, in suit and tie, with a beard, performing in front of a blackboard. No loincloth, no charisma, no awed disciples. Just an ordinary 1980s American guru.

guts.   In Victorian times, any possible reference to the human body was carefully avoided. That's why people spoke of piano limbs instead of legs.

Now we've come full circle and use the body—or parts of it—to mean abstract and intangible qualities.

A classic example was in William Safire's column (*New York Times,* 11/29/82). He wrote admiringly of the "brains and guts" of Mrs. Jeane Kirkpatrick, U.S. Ambassador to the United Nations.

Brains, used here to mean intelligence, actually refers to the gray matter we carry in our heads.

Guts, used to mean courage, fortitude, perseverance, stamina, is simply the English word for bowels, going back to the year 1000. *Guts* has been used as a slang word for daring and energy since 1893. The *Oxford English Dictionary* has a long string of respectable literary quotes from J. B. Priestley to John Cowper Powys to show the word's good standing.

Still and all, the word remains a slang word and probably always will be. The connection between lack of courage and bowel movements is too obvious to be overlooked.

So the word is slang. Which doesn't mean you shouldn't use it in a respectable context. Safire is an excellent writer and seems to have *carte blanche* from his employer, the *New York Times.* If he wants to say of a lady that she has brains and guts, more power to him.

guy.   On November 5, 1605, Guy Fawkes tried to blow up the British House of Lords. He was hanged, but became immortal. Every year on November 5 there is a parade in London in which an effigy of Guy Fawkes is carried through the streets. Then there are fireworks and children go around asking for "a penny for the guy"—sort of a British "trick or treat" custom.

Anyway, in the 1890s it dawned on the English-speaking people that the language lacked an anonymous word for an unspecified man—*fellow* just didn't satisfy—and so the word *guy* came into popular use. First it was considered slang, then it became "informal," and now it's highly printable and found just about everywhere.

In the *New York Times* (10/22/82) a diplomat was quoted as commenting on United Nations parties: "After you've seen the same guys at four parties in the same week, they begin to pall."

The *Nation* (10/30/82) wrote about the campaign of George Nicholson in California: "In his messianic fervor Nicholson sees only white and black, good guys and bad guys."

The *New Republic* (11/15/82) commented on the proposed Reciprocal Trade and Investment Act: "'Reciprocity' means you're only imposing your trade restrictions as a way to get the other guy to drop his."

Newsweek (11/8/82) wrote about the Sandinista rulers in Nicaragua: "By example, if nothing else, they pose a threat to right wing rulers in places like Honduras and Guatemala— bad guys, to be sure, but *our* bad guys."

So the word *guy,* meaning a man, has become fully established. But even that enormously broad meaning has been extended. *Guy* now means not only man, but man-or-woman. In the *New York Times Magazine* (10/24/82), President Reagan is quoted as telling a staff meeting: "You know, everybody in the press says that you guys have a conspiracy to talk me into a tax increase." History doesn't record whether there were women in the room, but it's certainly possible.

You guys is now the popular plural of *you.*

hairy. The *New York Times* (2/24/83) ran a lengthy piece on young married couples living with their in-laws. "If I stayed there longer, I'd have an ulcer," one young husband was quoted as saying. "We paid no rent, but that meant we became like a maid and butler. It was kind of hairy. It's not that you don't love each other, it's just that it's hard to be married and someone's child at the same time."

I tried to pin down the exact meaning of *hairy* in this slang sense. The regular dictionaries say, "presenting high risk or challenge, rugged, difficult, frightening, distressing, harrowing, hazardous."

That's clear enough, but where does that meaning come from? What has all this to do with hair? I dug further and found, in the *Dictionary of American Slang,* another set of adjectives—"dangerous, treacherous, tortuous, exciting, challenging." The dictionary adds: "said of an assignment, task, situation, etc.; of a place, such as a battlefield, racetrack, etc." This checked with one of the quotes given in the *Supplement to the Oxford English Dictionary.* It's from the astronaut Donald Slayton: "If you happen to be pulling a lot of Gs . . . it might get a little hairy trying to manipulate the controls with all the finesse you'd need."

I conclude from all this that *hairy* refers to the *terrain,* the situation you're up against, the tortuous track you're trying to follow. It calls for extreme skill, like piloting an airliner in a blizzard.

Or like living with your parents-in-law under one roof.

hang in there.   "Hang in there," wrote John J. O'Connor in the *New York Times* (1/4/83) about a TV movie. "It begins in a singles bar. Suggestion: Hang in there, the rest is all uphill."

This is a rather trivial use of the idiom *hang in there.* It means more than just *wait*—much more. It's one of the great recent inventions of the English language.

Up to about fifteen years ago, *hang in there* didn't exist and wasn't listed in any reference book. Then, suddenly, it sprang out of nowhere and was used by everyone.

The *Barnhart Dictionary of New English Since 1963* (1973) was the first to list *hang in there,* with the simple definition "to hold on or hang on."

Next came the *Oxford American Dictionary* (1980), which said "to persist in spite of adversity."

Next, *American Heritage Dictionary* (1982): "to persevere despite difficulties; persist."

Finally, the *New York Times Everyday Dictionary* (1982): "keep on; persevere; don't give up."

Hang in there is one of the great creative idioms of the English language. Part of its mysterious power is that it doesn't make any sense. Why *hang?* And why *hang in* and not *hang on?* And where is *there?* It's one of those totally unfathomable expressions like *I couldn't help it* or *I shouldn't wonder if it didn't rain.* And yet, *hang in there* makes glorious sense when spoken at the right time and in the right spirit. It can offer moral sustenance, stoic philosophy or Zen-like acceptance.

Just hang in there. Something is going to turn up. The Marines will land. A check will arrive in the mail. God will arrange one of His helpful miracles.

hang out.   The *Wall Street Journal* (12/30/82) ran an article about unemployment in Miami. "Estimates are," the article said, "that nearly 70% of Liberty City's young blacks are without work. They hang out at the busy intersection on 'miracle mile.'"

The quote pinpoints the exact meaning of the word *hang out.* Basically, to *hang* means to dangle, to be attached to a certain spot. If you *hang in there*, you stay put and don't move. But if you *hang out*, you dangle freely somewhere out-side—you loaf, you loiter, you idle away your time. To *hang out*, therefore, means to stay away from your work—or to *have* no work—to spend your time *not working*.

A *hangout*, which may be a neighborhood bar, is a place where people spend their leisure time. This applies even to the idle rich, who are said to *hang out* at their luxury homes.

Some dictionaries miss that essential meaning of *hanging out* or *hangout*. The *American Heritage Dictionary*, for in-stance, defines a *hangout* as "a frequently visited place."

What's missing here is the sense of loose dangling, the es-cape or isolation from the world of work.

The essence of hanging out is not coming *to* a place, but staying *away* from it.

hangup. In a movie review in *The New Yorker* (11/29/82) Pauline Kael wrote about a director's "acceptance of the various characters' attitudes and hangups."

Hangup has an interesting history. Back in the 1960s it meant a psychological block, something inside that holds you back, an emotional disturbance that interferes with your life. Gradually, the word began to be used for *any* kind of trivial bother or worry, emotional or not.

In 1968 *Maclean's* magazine wrote about "that big hangup for drivers caught in traffic lineups—the overheated engine." In the same year the *Observer* wrote: "People have this hangup about art. A woman will worry for days about spend-ing money on a painting: is it a good investment, can she trust her own judgment? The same woman will spend $150 on a dress . . . without giving it a thought."

By now, the concept of *hangup* has broadened fantastically. Anything can be called a *hangup*—being behind in your rent, having a sick relative, being stuck in traffic, not liking liver, watching soap operas every day, being obsessively neat—anything. There's nothing too big or too small to be called a *hangup,* with the implication that it will soon pass and a solution will be found.

In that movie reviewed in *The New Yorker,* the heroine's hangup was lesbianism combined with an overpowering desire to bear a child.

hanky.   Can you use the word *hanky* in writing?

The *Dictionary of American Slang* says it's used mainly by women. The *Supplement to the Oxford English Dictionary* calls it a "nursery and colloquial name for *handkerchief.*"

Hanky has been used since 1895. The quotes given in the *Oxford English Dictionary* show no distinction as to sex or age. Even if *hanky* was originally used by women and comes out of the nursery, it's now being used by everyone. Anyway, *handkerchief* is a long and elaborate word for a little thing like a hanky. A kerchief is a cover *(ker)* for the head *(chief).* Does it make any sense to speak of a handkerchief? It does not. *Handkerchief* is a word for department stores, but not for people.

It seems to me that *hanky,* like *pinkie,* has graduated and is now a word for mature men and women.

Recently (12/20/82) I read in *Newsweek:* "As Elliott in *E.T.,* actor Henry Thomas, 11, proved awfully adept at tugging on heartstrings, and it looks as if he's making another three-hanky movie, playing a boy whose mother dies, in *Misunderstood.*"

Should *Newsweek* have said "three-handkerchief movie"? Don't be absurd.

harrumphment. Is there such a word as *harrumphment?*

Yes. It was coined on December 20, 1982, by John J. O'Connor of the *New York Times.* Writing about a TV production of Shakespeare's *Cymbeline,* he mentioned the weird contrivances of the plot and wrote, "It is not surprising that Dr. Johnson, rising to harrumphment heights, declared: 'To remark the folly of the fiction, the absurdity of the conduct, the confusion of the names and manners of different times, and the impossibility of the events in any system of life, were to waste criticism upon unresisting imbecility, upon faults too evident for detection and too gross for aggravation.'"

I checked *harrumphment* in all dictionaries but couldn't find it anywhere. They list only *harrumph,* which means a clearing of the throat expressing disapproval. *Harrumphment* carries the pomposity one step further.

Thank you, John J. O'Connor. You've enriched the English language.

heck. Writing about the New York governor's race between Mario Cuomo and Lewis Lehrman, the *Newsweek* columnist George Will wrote (10/25/82): "For Cuomo, a former baseball player, politics is a long season, and you don't play with your teeth clenched. Heck, the team with the best record in baseball this year got beaten 67 times."

Heck is a venerable euphemism for *hell,* first used way back in 1887. Some dictionaries say *heck* is derived from the Scottish dialect word *hech,* a variant of *heigh,* which is an exclamation of surprise, sorrow, pleasure, fatigue or what-have-you. Other dictionaries confess that they don't know the origin of the word and simply say it's a euphemistic alteration of *hell,* expressing annoyance, rejection or disgust. *Most* dictionaries agree that *heck* is colloquial or informal.

Not so. *Heck,* that relic of the mid-Victorian times, is strictly a literary word. Few people *say* "heck." It's used almost solely by writers who are too timid to put the word *hell* on paper. *Heck* has been found in Sinclair Lewis's *Babbitt,* in *Studs Lonigan* by James T. Farrell, and—how literary can you get?—in Ezra Pound's translation of Sophocles' ancient Greek tragedy *Women of Trachis.* The exact quote reads: "That fellow was lying one time or the other. One heck of a messenger!"

By now, *heck* is an anachronism. These are no times for coy euphemisms. If you want to write *hell,* write *hell.* To hell with *heck.*

heist.   *Heist* is a perfect example of a word branded as slang in all dictionaries, but used quite freely in newspapers and magazines. *Newsweek* (12/27/82) described a robbery in the Bronx this way: "Thieves broke through the sheet-metal and tar-paper roof, handcuffed a lone guard and snatched $9.8 million—the biggest cash heist in U.S. history."

Back in the twenties *heist* was confined to underworld lingo and hardly known to the general public. But by 1947 it was respectable enough for a joke by the humorist S. J. Perelman in his book *Westward Ha!:* "His new ballpoint fountain pen had been heisted by the attendants."

Heist has become a word in general use *because* it is generally felt to be slang. It still has the power to give a nice tingle to law-abiding citizens, who know about armed robberies only through TV, newspapers and detective stories.

The word disproves the widely held notion that slang words

should be avoided in writing. Why deprive ourselves of a word that has such pleasantly exciting overtones?

hell.   Richard L. Strout, the famous "TRB" columnist of the *New Republic,* wrote (12/31/82): "Martin Feldstein, the new chairman of President Reagan's Council of Economic Advisers . . . is telling us that America and the world at Yuletide are in a hell of a mess."

What did he mean by *hell?* Obviously he wasn't referring to fire and brimstone or to the underworld or to damnation for eternity. The word *hell* has long ago lost its frightfulness. In fact, it has become the symbol of mildness. You can hardly say anything more *un*frightening than "a hell of a mess."

You could use the adjectives *miserable* or *wretched* or *dreadful* or *god-awful* or *disgusting* or *sickening* or *nauseating* or *revolting* or *repugnant* or *unbearable* or *intolerable* or *agonizing* or *tragic* or *heartbreaking* or *rotten* or *stinking.* Each one of these and dozens of other words are stronger than *hell of a.*

To say that things are in a hell of a mess is just about the mildest expression you can use. It actually minimizes the problem and treats it as a sort of joke.

Considering the fact that the world *is* in a very bad mess and that economists are wholly unable to solve the problem, use of the words *hell of a* is the ultimate understatement.

hit list.   The *New York Times* (1/14/83) said that General Charles A. Gabriel, one of the Joint Chiefs of Staff, told reporters the Chiefs preferred a cut in weapons purchases to a pay freeze. He added smilingly, "I'm not going to give you a hit list."

The slang phrase *hit list* is so new that it was in none of the regular desk dictionaries before the *American Heritage Dictionary,* which was published in 1982. There *hit list* was defined as "1. A list of potential murder victims as drawn up by a crime syndicate. 2. A list designating a target, as for attack, coercion, or elimination: *"had a hit list of executives he wanted fired."*

Hit list is an excellent example of the lightning speed with which slang gets accepted as standard English. First, in the 1950s, there was the word *hit,* used by criminals to mean a planned killing. A few years later there was *hit man,* a hired killer. Then, in the 1970s, there was the *hit list,* the list given to the hired killer of the people he was supposed to murder. Finally, in the late 1970s, there was the *hit list* in general, meaning any list of projects to scrap or people to fire.

What with TV and the movies, underworld slang nowadays becomes known to the public almost instantly. As I am writing (early 1983), *hit list* is just a phrase like any other used with no consciousness that it's slang or that it has anything to do with murder.

On the contrary, General Gabriel used *hit list* to mean a list of murderous weapons *not* to be used.

hock. The standard English word for pledging something as security for a debt is *pawn.* But people don't use that formal word. For well over a hundred years they've been using the slang word *hock* instead. Not only that, they're using the expression *in hock* whenever they're in debt, have bills to pay or are on the minus side financially.

Hock comes from the Dutch word *hok,* which means hutch,

hovel, prison. *Hock* originally was pure underworld slang, but so many people are poor or in debt that the word *hock* came into general use. *(Hock* is a debtors' word; *pawn* is a creditors' word.)

Among the literary quotes given in the *Supplement to the Oxford English Dictionary* is a sentence from a letter by the great American writer Jack London, written in 1898: "I got my watch out of hock."

The *New York Times* has given *hock* its stamp of approval. On January 25, 1983, the columnist Sydney Schanberg wrote, "The President, as you know, has been exhorting all Americans to help get the Federal Government out of hock by reaching deeper into their pockets and doing more 'voluntarism.'"

So don't use *pawn* or *debt*—use *hock.* Be human.

hogging. In an article on cancer research in the *New York Times Magazine* (10/24/82) there appeared the sentence "Until very recently, interferon seemed to hog the scientific limelight." Obviously, the authors of that article had no idea that they were smuggling an out-and-out slang word into the chaste pages of the *Times Magazine.*

The word *hogging* goes back to the 1880s and, for most people, has lost all connections with its intensely rural roots. People use it all the time when they mean selfish and greedy behavior. The picture of hogs around a trough, pushing and shoving to get their snouts into it, is not even faintly in people's minds. Most of those who write about hogging have never seen a hog's trough or a hog.

As I said, the word is a hundred years old and was used, among others, by Mark Twain in *Huckleberry Finn.* But according to the dictionaries, it has never become standard English. Why not? Probably because it's so mean and dirty that it seems to resist sanitizing. Even if it's innocent interferon that's hogging the limelight, it just isn't a pretty picture.

The New Yorker has a little newsbreak department that's called "Block That Metaphor!" I guess *hogging* is one of the most unblockable metaphors in the English language.

hokey.   Back in the 17th century jugglers used a faked Latin chant to divert their audience while they performed their tricks. The opening words were always "hocus pocus," which became the general word for trickery, deception, and sleight of hand. In the course of time this was shortened to *hokum,* and *hokum* in time was made into the adjective *hokey. Hokey* is slang, but reviewers use it freely whenever they spot anything contrived.

On Saturday, January 29, 1983, the *New York Times* entertainment guide listed a TV showing of the 1953 Marilyn Monroe movie *Niagara.* The description read: "Murderous cunning on honeymoon lane. Well-knit, engrossing thriller, one of Marilyn's best. Only lump is that hokey wind-up."

I'd never seen the movie, so I followed the recommendation of the *Times* and watched it. It was excellent, but the ending was indeed hokey. It showed a last-split-second helicopter rescue from certain death going down the falls.

I can hardly imagine anything more contrived. A classic instance of a cheap thrill.

There was no better word for it than *hokey.*

hooked.   The *New Republic*'s "TRB" columnist wrote (11/8/82) about the failure of the Penn Square Bank of Oklahoma City: "Penn Square's tangled finances included three hundred loans worth a billion dollars picked up by Chicago's Continental Illinois; it had gotten hooked on oil."

Hooked, of course, originally referred to a fish caught by an angler. In the 1940s drug abuse became so common that the most common meaning of *hooked* changed to *drug-addicted.* Finally *hooked* got to mean any kind of addiction to a person, cause or thing. And so we now have banks hooked on oil.

In 1965 the British journal the *New Statesman* wrote about being hooked on the city of Liverpool. In 1967 the *New Scientist* magazine wrote about people hooked on tobacco. In 1970 the London newspaper *Daily Telegraph* wrote, "Hundreds of domestic pets die each year after becoming hooked on slug bait."

Hooked has come a long way since 1653, when Izaak Walton wrote that most serene of all books, *The Compleat Angler or the Contemplative Man's Recreation.*

hopefully.   Flora Lewis, the foreign affairs columnist of the *New York Times,* wrote (12/14/82): "International Monetary Fund resources are to be enlarged, hopefully by at least 50 percent."

This is the use of the word *hopefully* purists have been struggling against for years. *Hopefully,* they say, means "in a hopeful manner." If you use it to mean "it is hoped; if all goes well," you've used it "incorrectly" and have committed a great crime against the English language.

That's sheer nonsense. The fact is that for centuries people who mentioned plans for the future habitually inserted the little phrase "God willing" to acknowledge their dependence on divine providence. In the past fifty or hundred years that pious phrase fell into disuse and people substituted the handy word *hopefully*. It follows the model of the German word *hoffentlich* and serves the same purpose.

After a quarter century of furious struggle, the purists have been roundly defeated. The use of *hopefully* in the sense of "if all goes well" is now universal. It is listed as standard usage in all four of the major desk dictionaries, without being labeled either informal or slang.

It's an established, accepted, often needed English word. Don't shy away from it.

hot potato. Hedrick Smith, the *New York Times* Washington bureau chief, recently (1/7/83) used the slang phrase *hot potato*. It was picked up for the headline of his article:

A Hand Reaches for Hot Potato of Social Security

I don't have to tell you what *hot potato* means. It's been used commonly for the past thirty-odd years. What did people say before? I started wondering.

I came to the conclusion that there just wasn't any expression that said exactly what is covered and implied by *hot potato*. The closest I could come was "Pandora's box"—which doesn't at all mean the same thing.

Anyway, you can hardly use "Pandora's box" nowadays—even the well-off, expensively educated readers of the *New York Times* mightn't know enough about Greek mythology to identify Pandora, the woman who was given a mysterious box and told not to open it. She promptly did and let out all the evils that have since beset mankind.

Greek mythology, which once supplied hundreds of metaphors and images for educated speakers and writers, has long fallen by the wayside. You couldn't casually mention "between Scylla and Charybdis," even, say, in the rarefied pages of the *New York Review of Books*. Better make it "between a rock and a hard place."

Beware of Greek mythology. It doesn't fly anymore.

humongous.   This is possibly the newest word listed in this book.

You won't find it in any of the standard desk dictionaries except *American Heritage* (1982) and *Webster's Collegiate* (1983). It's also in the 1980 *Oxford American Dictionary.* The *Oxford American* says it means tremendous and comes from a combination of *huge* and *enormous. American Heritage* and *Webster's* say it means enormous and comes perhaps from an alteration of *huge* and *tremendous.* All three of course call the word slang.

It's a lovely word. It's one of those prize examples of American flair for new words. The late H. L. Mencken, author of *The American Language,* would have treasured it. It was first found in print in 1976, barely seven years ago. Nobody knows who coined it. My guess is that maybe late at night, after a few beers, some witty, playful person in a bar in Boise, Idaho, let the word spring from his or her lips, feeling that *huge* was much too short a word for something that's super-enormous. The person sitting next to him or her picked it up, and then another and another and another and pretty soon the word, quite literally, spread.

By now every one of the 230 million American people knows what *humongous* means.

The *New York Times* (11/21/82) carried a long story about pregnant Mexican women who cross the Texas border to have their babies in the United States, letting them grow up as U.S. citizens.

Dr. Jesus Caquias, director of the Brownsville Community Health Clinic that employs six trained midwives, is quoted as saying, "It's a humongous problem and it's gotten worse."

I hear you say, that's quoted speech. It's not the language of *Times* staff members. It doesn't count.

My answer is that it does. Modern journalism aims for a maximum of quoted answers to interviewers. Dr. Caquias is not an illiterate yokel using unacceptable slang, but a man with a college education, a medical degree and a responsible position. If the *Times* reporter quoted him verbatim, he did so because he knew that all *Times* readers understand the word *humongous.*

Within ten years it'll appear in the staff-written text of the paper.

hype. The *New York Times* (1/6/83) wrote about the "behind-the-scenes hustle and hype of the pop-music game."

Hype has a fascinating history. It started around 1910 as a simple shortened word for a hypodermic needle. Then it became the word for hypodermic injection, particularly of a stimulant. By the 1960s it had become a metaphor for any kind of "deception, cheating, confidence trick, racket, swindle, or publicity stunt." That's how the *Supplement to the Oxford English Dictionary* puts it, and you can see clearly how the sense of the word gradually changed from a criminal act to a legal publicity stunt.

In 1968 the London *Sunday Times* explained *hype* to its English readers: "Hype is an American word for the gentle art of getting a tune into the pop charts without actually selling any records. Its methods are various, from the crudest bribery to devious techniques for upsetting the calculations of chart-compilers."

Now *hype* is entrenched as part of our culture. We all accept it. We know it's being done, but we no longer mind. Once these things were considered crimes and those who committed them were liable to be punished. Not anymore.

Hype now means socially accepted fraud.

iffy. President Franklin D. Roosevelt is usually credited with coining the word *iffy,* which means full of ifs. It sounds like him. The great pragmatist would naturally hesitate to predict the result of any proposal or the answer to any question. His approach was, Let's first try it and find out.

I found *iffy* in *Newsweek* (1/17/83). They ran a long article called "Portrait of America" and included a section on the future. It was titled "A Clouded Crystal Ball" and said, in a subhead, "All projections, by definition, are iffy."

Isn't *iffy* a lovely word? It's so American, so pragmatic, so unwilling to rely on hypotheses and theory. Projections are iffy, so is life, so is planning, so is everything.

The dictionary definitions of *iffy* are full of words like hypothetical, contingencies, conditions, doubts, uncertainties, unknown qualities, unresolved points or questions, or what-have-you. Roosevelt, or whoever it was, cut through all those Gordian knots and said the thing was iffy.

Well, the New Deal got established and worked. So did the word *iffy.*

in. A long headline over an article in the *New York Times* (11/19/82) read:

In Iran, Bravado Is In While Fear Is Everywhere

This sounded a little strange. The word *in*—in the sense of fashionable—is an old idiom, but usually refers to items of clothing, restaurants, and so on. "Turbans are in this year." "This is now the in place to eat." But bravado? Is bravado an item of passing fashion?

I studied the article and found that it described the current situation in Iran, with armed guards and barbed wire everywhere, but a pervasive underlying fear that the country can't go on forever defying the West.

Somewhere in the article the reporter wrote: "There is an approved Islamic look. Beards and fatigue jackets or windbreakers are in; neckties are out, a symbol of Western decadence."

This was the paragraph the headline writer picked to build his headline, applying "in-ness" to "bravado."

Well, yes, I suppose it's a possible way of putting it, and it does make for a snappy headline. But somehow I get the feeling that the headline writer didn't quite know what he meant to say. Did he try to make fun of the fierce Iranian Revolutionary Guards? Or did he consider submachine guns items of apparel?

into.   Recently (1/29/83) the *Nation* reviewed a book by a Jew who had been brought up as an agnostic and had returned to Orthodox Judaism. The reviewer didn't take much stock in his conversion. "After all," he wrote, "today's therapy is tomorrow's old news. Right now, I'm into Judaism. Tomorrow I may give yoga a shot. The day after, maybe I'll look into computers."

I guess that's the way many people feel about the slang expression *into*. It means, according to the *Barnhart Dictionary of New English Since 1963*, "to be deeply involved or interested in." But the question is, *how* deeply? If a person gets *into* something—say, astrology or Zen—there's always the implication that he or she will sooner or later get out of it.

If you're born a Catholic and stay a Catholic all your life, it does *not* mean that you're into Catholicism. Most likely, you're more lukewarm and casual about it than a convert who came to Catholicism later in life. But then, the convert, who got into it with a strong, driving conviction, is more apt to lose it later on.

That's why *into* always sounds a little ironic. You may say you're into whatever it is, but your friends will smile.

jerk. In the fall of 1982 *The New Yorker* ran one of its famous book-length articles, "Politics and Money" by Elizabeth Drew.

Writing in the best, meticulously crafted *New Yorker* style, Ms. Drew surveyed the whole landscape of the use of money to influence elections. At one point in the article, she admits that "not everyone who spends more money wins. Of course not; there are numerous factors in a campaign, ranging from the state of the economy to what might be termed the 'jerk factor'—having to do with the quality of the candidates."

"The jerk factor"! Searching for the exact word for what she wanted to say, Ms. Drew fell back on the universally known slang word *jerk.* A jerk is, as the unabridged *Webster's Third* says, "a stupid, foolish, naïve or unconventional person." No matter how much money you collect for his campaign, he'll make boo-boos, tell racial jokes, betray total ignorance of important matters, have skeletons in his closet.

He'll tell lies about his military or career record, he'll cheat on his income tax, he's been arrested for drunk driving, he's flunked exams, his life is a long chain of embarrassing stupidities.

As the German playwright Friedrich Schiller said, "Against stupidity even the gods fight in vain."

jinx.   You'll be as surprised as I was to learn where the word *jinx* comes from. I had assumed it was a rather recent slang word but found out that it goes back to antiquity. It belongs with pagan rites and the ancient elements of witch-craft.

A *jinx* (formerly spelled *jynx)* is a wryneck bird, a kind of woodpecker. Since ancient times, a wryneck was part of the recipe for a witches' brew, and this was widely known. *(Jynx* was the name of the wryneck in ancient Greece.)

The word appeared for the first time in a 1693 translation of Rabelais. (It had been used before to mean the bird, but in the Rabelais opus it was first used to mean a bad-luck spell.)

Ever since, *jinx* has been used innumerable times to mean a bad-luck charm, a curse, harmful magic that has evil effects. Probably because of this highly unsavory meaning, *jinx* has never been accepted by the purists as standard English and has been duly marked "informal" in the dictionaries. People ought to feel ashamed of using a word that embodies such unenlightened superstitions.

Nevertheless, the front page of the *New York Times* (12/5/82) reported that after Senator Kennedy's declaration that he wouldn't run for President in 1984, former Vice-President Walter Mondale expressed "indifference to the view that a jinx goes with an early lead in nomination contests."

So nowadays the *Times* is no longer afraid of the word *jinx.* Or of a jinx itself.

jock.   In *Newsweek*'s "Periscope" section (11/15/82) I read about a forthcoming two-hour NBC TV movie based on the popular commercials for Miller Lite beer. "It will be much more than lots of jocks making lots of jokes in lots of bars."

A jock, as everyone knows, is a male athlete. Where does the word come from? All dictionaries agree that it's an abbreviation of *jockstrap,* which means an elastic supporter for the genitals. Athletes were kiddingly called *jockstraps,* and later just *jocks.*

Jock is a word with an undertone of good-natured mild fun. An example of that attitude is this quote by Dan Wakefield *(Atlantic,* July 1969): "The only funny performance is by Michael Meyer as Brenda's jock brother, a big, gregarious, simple-minded, good-hearted lug who has exactly the right moves of the athlete—shoulder-rolling, ass-slapping, gum-chewing—all down pat."

In 1972 *Webster's New World Dictionary* defined *jockstrap* or *jock* as "an athlete; often a derogatory term." That feeling seems to have evaporated. The 1982 *American Heritage Dictionary* simply says, "a male athlete, esp. in college."

However, there's an interesting added definition: "One characterized by excessive concern for machismo."

john.   Charlotte Curtis, the society reporter of the *New York Times,* wrote the other day (12/28/82) about a private dinner at which former Secretary of State Haig was the guest of honor. He told about the trip to Anwar Sadat's funeral when three former Presidents rode together on Air Force One.

"There was only one stateroom," Haig said. "So, being a diplomat, I took it. There were plenty of johns but Carter wanted to use mine. I finally locked the door on him."

Telling this anecdote at a fancy dinner table surrounded by Washington bigwigs, Haig used the word *john.* He didn't say *rest room* or *lavatory* or *bathroom.* The word that sprang to his lips in those elegant surroundings was *john.*

Apparently *john* is now the common American term. You'll be surprised to learn that it first appeared in print in a 1735 Harvard regulation that said, "No Freshman shall . . . go into the Fellows' cus John." (*Cus* meant *cousin.*) Why "Cousin John," nobody knows.

Of course we have oodles of euphemisms—*toilet, rest room, comfort station.* The British say *W.C.* (water closet). The French, being realists, say *pissoir.*

The other day I heard a woman say on television that she was taking her dog outdoors to go to the bathroom.

We're a funny people, speaking a funny language.

junk food.   *Junk food* appeared in the *New York Times* twice on the same day (10/7/82). An article on life in Japan said that "Japanese youngsters have rushed headlong into the world of American fast foods, junk foods and sugar-rich items." On another page an article dealing with the new national newspaper *USA Today* said, "Some dismiss it, with its flood of short articles, as journalistic junk food."

What exactly is junk food? In October 1982 it was not listed in any of the major dictionaries. I had to go to the *Second Barnhart Dictionary of New English* to find it. Its first occurrence in print was in 1973.

Where does *junk food* come from? It's a long story. First, back in 1485, junk meant old pieces of rope (derived from a Portuguese word). Gradually, in the 19th century, *junk* was used to mean any kind of scrap or waste material that could be put to use. Finally, *junk* was used for any kind of worthless trash.

Junk food is defined as "quickly prepared and ready-made, often containing a large proportion of food substitutes, and usually rich in carbohydrates, such as imitation potato chips."

You might as well eat old pieces of rope.

junkie.   On December 10, 1982, the *New York Times* ran an article by its White House correspondent Francis X. Clines about President Reagan's Director of Communications, David R. Gergen.

Gergen, Clines wrote, loved to discuss political issues with the press. He was "an issue junkie. He ingests them easily as the little cookies that he orders from the White House mess in the evenings."

For all I know, this was the first time the slang word *junkie* was used casually in the pages of the *Times*. If so, December 10, 1982, was something of a historical landmark, a cultural signpost. *Junkie* has now become a standard everyday word, to be used without any connotations of crime, danger or tragedy.

The word has come a long way. Back in the twenties it began to be used to mean a drug addict. Gradually it became more widely known. In 1951, the *New York Times* felt it had to give its readers the following elaborate explanation: "An addict who sells narcotics, for which he usually gets his own daily supply, is called a 'junkie' . . . and they hang out in taverns and cafes until the police raid them."

During the sixties and seventies drug abuse became immensely widespread and *junkie* became, unhappily, a household word. Not only that, it was used more and more not only for a drug addict or pusher, but for any kind of fan. By 1982, the second college edition of the *American Heritage Dictionary* defined *junkie* this way: "*Slang*. 1. A narcotics addict, esp. one using heroin. 2. One who has an avid interest or devotion: *a sports junkie.*"

kibitz.   Whenever a language has no word for a frequently recurring situation, it invents a new one.

The Jews have been cardplayers for many centuries. They noted that there was always some onlooker behind one or another of the players, giving unwanted advice on game strategy and tactics, and bothering everybody.

Finally somebody thought of a name for this kind of person. The word inventor was reminded of a European bird, called *kiebitz* in German and *kibitz* in Yiddish, that was famous for its shrill, unpleasant cry. (The word *kibitz* imitates the cry, as does the word *peewit* for the related American bird.) The picture was clear: the unshushable spectator resembled a kibitz, perched on the shoulder of a player and endlessly uttering his painfully annoying cries.

Imported to America, *kibitz* became the word for the activity, and *kibitzer* the word for the culprit.

It's not a slang word. Some dictionaries mark it as informal. Recently (*New York Times,* 12/2/82) it appeared as a standard English word in a book review about the early Jewish immigrants in New York City. There was a reference to "the famous kibitzing waiters at Ratner's dairy restaurant."

There are few words in the English language that pack such a colorful metaphor and such a wealth of specific meaning.

kibosh.   "Not since antitrust spoilsports put the kibosh on the Gilded Age has an American capitalist reveled so openly in the pleasures that money can buy," wrote the *New Republic* (8/16/82), quoting *People* magazine on the publisher Malcolm Forbes.

Kibosh is an intriguing word. You can pronounce it either KYbosh or kiBOSH. *Putting the kibosh on* means to check, stop, block. But where does the word come from? It's a great mystery.

The unabridged *Webster's Third* says, with its customary caution, "origin unknown." The unabridged *Random House* says simply "?" The *Oxford English Dictionary* says "Origin obscure" and adds skeptically, "It has been stated to be Yiddish or Anglo-Hebraic." *Webster's New World* chimes in with "? Yid." Wentworth and Flexner's *Dictionary of American Slang* says unhesitatingly, "of Turkish origin." And the *Morris Dictionary of Word and Phrase Origins* says the Irish poet Padraic Colum thinks *kibosh* comes from the Gaelic *cie bais,* which means "cap of death."

I don't believe for a minute that *kibosh* comes from Yiddish. In the first place, *kibosh* has been used since the 1850s, long before the mass immigration of Yiddish-speaking Jews. In the second place, *kibosh* just doesn't sound Yiddish to me, in spite of the *k* and the *sh.*

Turkish, I would think, is quite out of the running. Why Turkish? Is there any word in Turkish that means anything like *kibosh?* And how would a Turkish word get rooted in American soil?

That leaves the Irish paternity claim of Padraic Colum. It rings true to me. I can even imagine, without too much strain, KYbosh or kiBOSH being spoken with an Irish brogue.

Anyway, what an extraordinary word!

kick.   The word *kick* has many meanings, most of them slang. Among other things, it means, according to Wentworth and Flexner's *Dictionary of American Slang,* "Anything that gives one a thrill, excitement, or satisfaction, ranging from violence, narcotics, whisky, and sex through jazz, books and art to food, dress, and sleep."

On December 30, 1982, Herbert Mitgang of the *New York Times* wrote about an exhibition of Anthony Trollope manuscripts at the Morgan Library on East 36th Street in Manhattan. He inteviewed Herbert Cahoon, the curator of autograph manuscripts.

Cahoon, living a sheltered life in a hushed environment, was not the kind of person one would expect to use slang. And yet, when Mitgang asked him whether he'd read all the Trollope material in the exhibition, he said yes, he had.

"But I don't think I've read more than a half-dozen of his novels," he added. "At the moment, I'm on a Balzac kick."

kid.   *The New Yorker,* that famous model of exquisite, carefuly edited prose, does not consider the use of the word *kid* for *child* in any way objectionable. On the contrary, it often prefers it. A 250-word article on video games (10/4/82) begins: "In the village of Ocean Beach, on Fire Island, kids under the drinking age spent most of their quarters this past summer . . ." In the rest of the article the words *kid* or *kids* appeared twenty-one times; the words *child* or *children* not once.

In everyday American speech *kid* or *kids* has now largely replaced *child* or *children.* Even young adults in their twenties and thirties are often called kids by their elders. Why? Because it's more personal, more affectionate, more intimate. *Child* or *children* is considered too stiff—too official—a word for filling out bureaucratic forms.

When was *kid,* the word for a young goat, first used to mean a child? In 1599, in a play by the Elizabethan playwright Philip Massinger. And yet, the almost 400-year-old usage is still only grudgingly recognized by our dictionaries. In *Webster's New World Dictionary* you find: *"kid.* 1. a young goat or, occasionally antelope. 2. its flesh, used as a food. 3. leather made from the skin of young goats, used for gloves, shoes, etc. 4. gloves or shoes made of this leather. 5. (*Colloq.*) a child or young person."

At least they don't call it slang anymore, like the 19th-century *Oxford English Dictionary.* But the primary meaning of *kid* for our dictionarymakers is still a young goat.

Or a young antelope.

kidding. Recently (1/12/83) Frank Rich, the theater critic of the *New York Times,* reviewed a new play, in which a daughter tells her mother that she's going to commit suicide. "At first," Rich wrote, the mother "prefers to disbelieve her ears, [but] her daughter isn't kidding."

Kidding is one of the most common words in our language, although most dictionaries still label it "informal" and deny it its place in the standard vocabulary. Originally, *kidding* meant behaving playfully like a little goat; gradually the meaning changed to bantering, teasing, joshing, jesting. The unabridged *Webster's Third* defines *kidding* as "to make fun of usu. good-humoredly and often by innocent deception." *Webster's New World* says "to tease or ridicule playfully."

The point about kidding is that it can't be done without a playful, good-humored attitude. Both kidder and "kiddee" must fully understand that no harm is meant. It's all in fun, a little game between equals.

Kidding is one of the basic social graces that pervade American life. Everybody is always kidding everybody else, as a sort of token of mutual acceptance and general good intentions.

Kidding is the mark of social democracy and reasonable equality. You can't kid anyone across a social gulf—he'll never be sure whether you perhaps meant seriously what you said.

Visitors from other countries are always amazed at the steady bantering and kidding that goes on among us—all of us, even members of different social classes and sometimes races.

Kidding is the great cement that holds American society together. It's one of the foundations of our democracy.

kinky.   A movie review in the *Nation* (11/6/82) says, "An impecunious couple . . . stumbles on the lucrative device of luring men, hungry for kinky sex, to their apartment. . . ."

Kinky goes back to the 1860s when it referred simply to closely curled hair. Around 1900 it began to be used figuratively in the sense of queer, eccentric, crochety. E. M. Forster wrote in 1907: "This jaundiced young philosopher, with his kinky view of life, was too much for him." In 1950 T. S. Eliot wrote in his play *The Cocktail Party:* "But when everything's bad form, or mental kinks, You either become bad form, and cease to care, Or else, if you care, you must be kinky."

As you see, until the 1950s, *kinky* was used without any reference to sex. Or, if it was used in its sexual sense, that sense didn't surface either in literature or in the dictionaries.

Then, almost suddenly, sex—all kinds of sex—became mentionable. Kinky sex became a household word. Today, kinky sex is openly acknowledged in all dictionaries. *Random House* says, "way-out, offbeat, or far-out, esp. sexually." *Webster's New World* says: "weird, bizarre, eccentric, peculiar, etc.; specif. sexually abnormal or perverse." *American Heritage* says: "a. Marked by or making use of a perverted eroticism. b. Marked by sexual perversion." *Webster's Colle-*

giate says "relating to, having, or appealing to bizarre or un-conventional tastes, esp. in sex; *also:* sexually deviant."

klutz.   The Paris correspondent of the *New York Times* (1/16/83) reported on a French government crisis. His piece began: "All of a sudden governments lose their touch. They bump into things, botch them. They slip on roller skates and knock over flower pots. Whether the cause of the trouble is important becomes secondary; to the public, the government looks like a klutz."

Klutz got into English only about ten or fifteen years ago. It comes from the Yiddish and is derived from the German word *Klotz*, which means a block of wood. So a *klutz* is clumsy and awkward, the kind of person who lacks natural grace.

In 1970 *Time* quoted the actress Candice Bergen: "Basically I'm the klutz who makes a terrific entrance to the party and then trips and falls and walks around with food in her hair."

The thing about *klutz*, like most Yiddish words, is that it's a kind, sympathetic word. After all, if you're a klutz, it's not your fault. It's the way God made you. Not everyone can be an athlete and shine on the tennis court or the ski slopes. A klutz may have other redeeming qualities—intelligence, for ex-ample.

knee-jerk.   If you look up *knee jerk* in *Webster's Third* unabridged dictionary, you'll find this: "an involuntary for-ward jerk or kick induced by a light blow or sudden strain upon the patellar tendon of the knee that causes a reflex con-traction of the quadriceps muscle."

Like most people, you've probably had the experience of

having your reflexes tested by a doctor and watched the funny kick of the leg that you couldn't control.

In 1963, two years after the publication of *Webster's Third,* the knee jerk appeared for the first time in print in its political sense. The *New York Times* reported on "knee-jerk liberals in Washington." Of course, what was meant was politicians whose liberal reactions were as automatic as the patellar reflex or knee jerk.

Since then, the term (listed in the *Dictionary of American Slang*) has been bandied about from right to left and back again from left to right. It's always meant as an insult.

On February 8, 1983, the *New York Times* carried an op-ed article by James Tobin, a Nobel prize winner in economics. Tobin expressed his faith in pump-priming to save the economy. He wrote: "The knee-jerk objection to the strategy is, 'It's inflationary.' This is really an objection to recovery itself."

Knee-jerk is a funny and highly expressive word—far better in this context than, say, *standard* or *automatic.*

laid-back. *Laid-back* is a slang word that was first sighted in print in 1969. According to the *Second Barnhart Dictionary of New English* (1980) it may have referred originally to a rider on a motorcycle who lies back on a long backrest. (Of course, most people would say "lays back.") Anyway, it means relaxed, easygoing, low-keyed, nonchalant. Like so many slang words, it conveys instantly what is meant.

I found an amusing example of *laid-back* in an article on skyscrapers in *Newsweek* (11/8/82). In a discussion of Chicago skyscrapers built by Bruce Graham, the article says, "The complex errs pleasantly on the side of comfortable dullness. . . . In its laid-back character, [it] clashes sharply with the theatrical razzle-dazzle of Graham's main competitors."

To call a group of skyscrapers "laid-back" is surely the height of something or other. And yet, the description seems to fit. You can see, in your mind's eye, Graham's unassuming towers contrasting with their vividly exciting neighbors.

Laid-back is a California-type word, whether it was actually coined there or not. But as you see, it can be transferred to Chicago.

laundering money.
Here's a case history of a slang word that made it into standard English. On November 17, 1982, a story in the *New York Times* carried the headline

Ring Is Smashed for 'Laundering' of Drugs Money

In the story, the word *launder* appeared between quotation marks and was carefully explained. *Laundering* meant funneling money from illegal sources through bank accounts that were then transferred to other states or countries. The "clean" money was then withdrawn by the payees.

A week later (11/24/82), there was another article on the same case. It carried the headline

Laundered Money Focus of Inquiries

The quotation marks around the word *laundered* had disappeared. Way down in the article there was a paragraph for the benefit of upstanding *Times* readers unfamiliar with underworld lingo: "Money is 'laundered' by moving it through various financial instruments and institutions that camouflage its origin or the identity of its owners. A drug dealer, for example . . ." etc.

As it happens, by the time the *New York Times* gave in to current English usage, laundering money was known to almost everybody in the United States. They'd learned all about it ten years ago, from the Watergate scandals.

lay. In *The New Yorker* (1/3/83) Berton Roueché told about his visit to Pratt, Kansas. He'd talked to Mr. Paul Epp, owner of Epp Coins & Supply, about coins and coin prospecting.

"It's interesting," Mr. Epp said, "what happens when you drop a coin. Most people think it sinks into the ground. Not at all. It lays there, and gradually the dust and dirt overlays it."

Roueché, who is an excellent writer, took down Mr. Epp's words exactly as he said them. He said "It lays there." He didn't say "It lies there."

I looked up *lay* in the four major American desk dictionaries. *Webster's Collegiate* says, *"nonstandard:* lie." *Random House College* says, *"nonstandard:* lie." *Webster's New World* says, "to lie; recline: a dialectal or substandard usage." *American Heritage* says, *"Nonstandard.* To lie."

So it's unanimous. To say *lay* instead of *lie* is "nonstandard" or "substandard."

"Nonstandard" means, according to *American Heritage,* "not acceptable to educated speakers. . . . Certain terms and expressions have never been admitted to the standard language." (*Substandard,* according to *Webster's New World,* means the same as *nonstandard.*)

The question is, admitted by whom? Answer: by the self-appointed guardians of "correct" English, the dictionary-makers.

This answer wasn't good enough for me, so I looked up *lay* in that monument of scientific research, the *Oxford English Dictionary.* There I found that *lay* has been used in the sense of *lie* since 1300. The long list of quotes includes Caxton ("His chief standards overthrown and laying upon the ground"), Fielding ("The flame which had before laid in embryo now burst forth"), and Byron ("Thou dashest him again to earth:—there let him lay").

I also looked up *lay* in the *Dictionary of Contemporary American Usage* by Bergen and Cornelia Evans, which is based on linguistic science. The Evanses say, "The verb *lay* . . . is defensible . . . in *he lays on the floor* or . . . *it is laying on the table.* Both verbs, *lay* and *lie,* are correct so far as theoretical grammar is concerned."

Never mind those snooty dictionarymakers. If it comes naturally to you to say or write "It lays there," do it.

You've almost seven hundred years of respectable usage behind you.

lemon.   The *Wall Street Journal* (1/21/83) ran a story about Al Jacobs, who helps people shop for a car for a $175 consultant fee.

"If he has a strong hunch about what he calls a model's 'lemon factor,' he advises against buying it," the *Journal* reported.

"The lemon factor"! Of course you know what Jacobs meant by that. But could you define it? I looked up the slang meaning of *lemon* in the four major desk dictionaries and found four different definitions. *Webster's New World* says, "something, esp. a manufactured article, that is defective or imperfect." *Random House College* says, "an inferior person or thing; dud." *Webster's Collegiate* says, "one (as an automobile) that is unsatisfactory or defective." *American Heritage* says, "one that is, or proves to be, unsatisfactory; washout."

The last definition, with the words "proves to be," contains the clue to the essential meaning of *lemon*. It's something you buy, take home and use—and *then,* to your intense disappointment, the damn thing doesn't work properly or not at all. It's like buying what you think is an orange, tasting it, and finding out it's a sour lemon.

In drafting a federal law, the lawyers, who had to be exact, found they had a problem when it came to defining a lemon. They solved it beautifully. Section 104 (a) (4) of the federal Magnuson-Moss Warranty Act—the "lemon provision"—says, that "if the product . . . contains a defect . . . after a reasonable number of attempts to remedy [it, the] warrantor must permit the consumer . . . either a refund or replacement without charge."

So if you've bought something with a warranty and it can't be fixed even though the company tried several times, they have to give you your money back or give you a new car, TV or whatever.

But the law doesn't make up for the pain you suffered in getting stuck with a lemon.

like.   The number one taboo of the purists is the use of *like* as a conjunction. Strunk and White's best-seller, *Elements of Style* (3d ed. 1979), says, "*Like.* Not to be used for the conjunction *as. . . . Like* has long been widely misused by the illiterate. . . . For the student, perhaps the most useful thing to know about *like* is that most carefully edited publications regard its use before phrases and clauses as simple error."

In the leading newspapers and magazines I've checked in compiling this book it's almost impossible to find *like* used instead of *as*—or *as if*—in the regular text. The rule has been drummed into the minds of editors and writers for too many decades.

But the other day it happened. On the op-ed page of the *New York Times* (12/9/82) there was a piece by Bernard Goldberg on the lack of courtesy in New York City. "[Toughness]," Goldberg wrote, "is part of the folklore of the city. But New Yorkers are tough only like the prisoners at Rikers Island are tough. . . ."

Hurray for Goldberg. He has broken through the great taboo. Of course, he's a correspondent for CBS News and used to spoken English rather than the artificial, carefully edited language of our top magazines and papers. *Like* instead of *as* comes naturally to him and he doesn't think twice in putting it on paper. Never mind those purists who can't stand the way America talks.

When it comes to spoken *like*—rather than *like* used in a prepared text—it can be found everywhere every day.

An unemployed steelworker staying home with the kids is quoted (*Wall Street Journal,* 12/8/82) saying, "I'm stuck here all day, and sometimes that feels like I'm in prison."

An importer of fancy Japanese clothes says (*Newsweek,* 11/8/82), "We don't sell Kawakubo clothes like we sell Armani."

The actor Paul Newman says (*Time,* 12/6/82), "My father treated me like he was disappointed in me a lot of the time."

And so it goes. All of us, in talking, use *like* instead of *as* or *as if.* It's the standard American idiom.

Six weeks after Bernard Goldberg broke through the great taboo on the op-ed page, the *Times* itself succumbed to the prevailing idiom. Staff reporter Michael Oreskes wrote from Albany (1/21/83): "The wind blasting in off the Hudson has made it feel like it is 35 below zero here."

literally.   On November 11, 1982, the *New York Times* reported on a government proposal to repair bridges and highways. Secretary of Transportation Drew Lewis was quoted as saying, "We have highways and bridges that are literally falling down around our ears."

This use of the word *literally,* in the sense of "figuratively," has been a pet peeve of language purists for many decades.

Fowler's *Modern English Usage* (2d ed.) says, "Such false coin makes honest traffic in words impossible."

Theodore M. Bernstein's *The Careful Writer* says, "What most writers (and speakers) mean when they use *literally* is *figuratively,* which is just about its opposite."

The Elements of Style by William Strunk Jr. and E. B. White (3d ed.) says, *"Literally.* Often incorrectly used in support of exaggeration or violent metaphor."

And the *American Heritage Dictionary* (2d college ed. 1982) contains the following usage note:

> Literally *means "in a manner that accords precisely with the words." It is often used to mean "figuratively" or "in a manner of speaking," which is almost the opposite of its true meaning. Thus, it is not correct to say* he was literally breathing fire *except when speaking of a dragon.*

The use of the word "correct" in this usage note is a dead giveaway. The purists, including the editors of the *American Heritage Dictionary,* still cling to the wholly outmoded concept of "correct English usage."

Literally in the sense of figuratively is an established English idiom that has been constantly used since 1863, when a British author wrote, "For the past four years, I literally coined money."

loaning. On January 3, 1983, the *New York Times* quoted the economist Alan Greenspan, who had appeared the day before on "Meet the Press." He had warned, "There are an awful lot of banks out there. Well over a hundred banks, for example, are loaning to Mexico."

The use of *loan* as a verb always was a red flag for the purists. By now most of them have given in, but three of the diehards are still holding out.

The Elements of Style by Strunk and White (3d ed. 1979) says, *"Loan.* A noun. As a verb, prefer *lend."*

The *Oxford American Dictionary* (1980) says, "Many writers prefer *lend* over *loan* as a verb."

And the *New York Times Manual of Style and Usage* (1976) says, *"loan.* Avoid as a verb; use *lend.* And *lent,* rather than *loaned."*

I wondered how long this "incorrect" usage has been followed. The *Oxford English Dictionary* gives two quotes from the 13th century, but isn't quite sure about the spelling. The first certain use of *loan* as a verb dates back to 1542. The pre-Shakespeare play *Henry VIII* contains the line "Loaning or laying out the same for gain in purchasing lands."

So *loan* as a verb has been standard English for at least 440 years.

loner.   *Newsweek* (11/8/82) described John Hinckley, the man who almost killed President Reagan, as "a deranged loner."

Loner has been in use for some thirty years. It means "one who avoids the company of others."

The *Dictionary of American Slang* by Wentworth and Flexner says that *loner* is used both as a complimentary word—meaning "one strong enough to get along without help"—and as a derogatory word—"an eccentric or unsociable person."

In theory that may be true, but in practice, I'm afraid, most people don't like or admire a loner. They distrust anyone who keeps aloof. Particularly in recent years, since a number of loners have killed or attacked public figures, the loner sends a shiver of fear through most people. What is he up to? Why does he keep to himself? Who knows, he may be another Lee Harvey Oswald or John Hinckley.

This seems to me unfair. There are introverts and extraverts among us, and we shouldn't be prejudiced against the unsociable. America has its Oswalds and Hinckleys, but it has also had its Thoreaus and Emily Dickinsons. Gregariousness is not necessarily a virtue and solitariness is no vice.

The person who hates to go to parties may prefer to stay home and write immortal poetry.

lousy.   You'll be interested to know that the word *lousy* is no longer slang. That is, *lousy* in the sense of bad, inferior, of poor quality.

To be sure, *lousy* used to be a slang word in that figurative sense, listed in the *Oxford English Dictionary* with the meaning of "mean, scurvy, sorry, vile, contemptible," with a string of quotes starting with one from Chaucer dated 1386 down to one from Robert Louis Stevenson dated 1893. But the *OED* article, written in the early 1920s, adds "Now rare."

But wait. In 1976, volume 2 of the *Supplement to the Oxford English Dictionary* was published. It said: "Delete 'Now rare' and add further examples. Also, inferior, poor, bad, ill; in low health or spirits." Then follow some twenty examples from various sources, including a poem by D. H. Lawrence.

The *Oxford English Dictionary* as of 1976 does *not* label *lousy* as slang. Nor does *Webster's Collegiate* (1983), *Random House College* (1975) or *American Heritage* (1982). (*Webster's New World* is the only holdout among the four major desk dictionaries.)

As for the *New York Times,* it now tolerates *lousy* if quoted from a respectable source. Helmut Sonnenfeldt, who served in the State Department under Nixon and Ford and still acts as a private adviser under Reagan, seems to have the proper credentials. He was quoted (11/16/82) as having said, "Soviet-American relations are lousy."

macho, machismo. Back in 1964 the English magazine *Punch* felt it had to explain the word *macho:* "A quality much prized in Mexico, namely 'masculinity,' 'virility.'"

In the twenty years since, *macho* and *machismo* have become common English words, used by everyone. *Time* magazine (1965) called *machismo* a "he-man complex that makes sexual prowess and large families—in or out of wedlock—a matter of male pride."

Lately the words *macho* and *machismo* have been used almost solely with skepticism and irony. Latin Americans may still believe in machismo, but we now seem to look at it as something of a quaint aberration.

In a review of Gabriel García Marquez's latest novel, Peter S. Prescott (*Newsweek,* 11/1/82) wrote: "García Marquez's target is the idiocy of machismo, the attitude that 'honor is love.'"

And in the *New York Times* (10/21/82) there was a revealing interview with Tom Hays, vice-president of the American Tobacco Company. The company was about to reintroduce Lucky Strike cigarettes. "The company tried a macho slant," the *Times* reported. "The problem here was its rivals were big on macho. Mr. Hays nodded at a Marlboro ad of a cowboy on a horse . . . and a Winston ad of two construction workers. He pointed to a Camel ad of a man wading through a stream. . . .

'How do you out-macho this?' he asked. 'You'd have to go to outright killers.'"

masterfully.   "The director, Tom Moore, has choreographed the action masterfully" (*New York Times,* 1/12/83).

What's wrong with this sentence? Purists will say it's the word *masterfully.* According to their rules, *masterful* means domineering; the word for expert is *masterly.* The *Times* reviewer should have written *masterly* or perhaps *masterlily.*

This nonsense goes back to H. W. Fowler's *Modern English Usage* (1926). Fowler said that centuries ago the two words were used interchangeably, but now, if someone doesn't use *masterful* in the sense of strong-willed and *masterly* in the sense of skillful, "it can only be put down to ignorance."

In the years since Fowler's famous book appeared, the purists have followed his lead like sheep. The *New York Times Manual of Style and Usage* (1976 edition) says with harsh certitude: "*masterful* (overpowering), *masterly* (skillful)."

The height of the purist disregard for natural idiom was reached by Theodore Bernstein's *The Careful Writer* (1965). "The distinction between *masterful* and *masterly* is worth preserving," he wrote. Then he went on to give advice on how to write à la Bernstein: "Although *masterly* is an adverb as well as an adjective, and although there is another adverbial form of it—*masterlily*—neither is completely satisfactory. 'He paints masterly' sounds just as odd as 'He paints masterlily.' Each requires rephrasing into something like, 'He paints in a masterly manner.'"

The chutzpah is staggering. Let me just add that *masterfully* in the sense of expertly or skillfully has been used since 1613. Never mind the antics of the purists.

maven. *Newsweek* (12/13/82) wrote about troubles of the Chock full o' Nuts restaurant chain. It said its TV commercials, sung by the company president's wife, "may not have impressed media mavens."

Maven, a Yiddish import into the English language, has an interesting history. In the 1960 edition of the *Dictionary of American Slang* it is listed with the spelling *mayvin* and defined as "a self-styled expert in man's clothing; a customer who professes to know more about tailoring styles, etc., than a clothing salesman." This was based on a single quote from an article in the *New York Times Magazine,* which appeared in 1952. The dictionary noted the word was "not common."

By 1975, when the supplement to the *Dictionary of American Slang* appeared, the situation had changed considerably. The word was now listed as *mavin* or *maven* (the current spelling has settled down to *maven*) and the tone was vastly more positive. A *maven* was now defined as "an expert or connoisseur in any field." A 1970 quote read: "There I was, happily schlepping pizzas to a steady and growing clientele of pizza mavins . . ."

Today, *maven* is in all the dictionaries. The best definition is that of *Random House:* "an expert, esp. in everyday matters." There are examples quoted of herring mavens, real estate mavens, boxing mavens, publishing mavens.

Maven comes, via Yiddish, from the Hebrew word for understanding. A maven is someone who understands, on the basis of unbeatable experience. In a court of law, a maven wouldn't be admitted as an expert witness, since he or she has no certificate or diploma, no degree, no academic tenure. A maven just *knows.*

miff. *Miff* is a very subtle word. It means to put into an ill humor; make peevish; offend; annoy. *A miff* is a petty quarrel, a tiff, a huff. Most dictionaries say the word imitates a cry of disgust.

So the word has an intimate, intensely personal connotation. It's something that happens in a living room, one step up from simply raising an eyebrow. A minor chilling of the atmosphere, within a small group.

The journalists, in their newfound freedom to use informal words, have latched onto *miff* and used it for public major quarrels, where it doesn't fit at all. The *New Republic* (11/29/82) wrote about the new Vietnam War Memorial in Washington, D.C. The original austere design, at the insistence of Vietnam veterans' organizations, was changed to include a flag and a sculpture of three soldiers. "These additions miffed the art community," the magazine said.

Miffed? The artists were outraged and infuriated. They considered the realistic additions sheer sacrilege and stirred up an awful row.

A few months later (1/12/83) the *Wall Street Journal* reported on the popularity of American country and western music in Poland. During the past year, ever since Poland had been put under martial law, country music clubs had been closed, radio programs went off the air, cutting albums became impossible, records, cassettes and songbooks disappeared from the stores.

And what was the headline the *Wall Street Journal* put out on this tale of government suppression and persecution?

Poles' Country Music Hails From Nashville
And Miffs Officials

mighty. In his classic book *The American Language* (1938) H. L. Mencken wrote: "Practically all the adverbs made from verbs with -y lose their terminal -ly and thus become identical with their adjectives. I have never heard *mightily* used; it is always *mighty* as in 'He hit him mighty hard.'"

The old master was quite right, except for one thing—this is not a special feature of the American language. It has been observed in British English since 1300. Dickens wrote in *Oliver Twist:* "This is all mighty fine."

The adverbial use of *mighty* is going as strong as ever. Just the other day, TV reviewer John J. O'Connor wrote in the *New York Times* (11/23/82): "Priscilla English's script sticks mighty close to the 'All About Eve' scenario."

You'd think that this tiny bit of "incorrect" English, entrenched in the language for almost seven hundred years, would have escaped the eagle eyes of the purists. Not at all. I quote from the *Harper Dictionary of Contemporary American Usage* (1975) by William and Mary Morris: *"Mighty,* in the sense of *very,* is heard in such phrases as a *'mighty* fine horse' and is an informal expression accepted in speech but to be avoided in writing, except where used to indicate character."

This ridiculous advice is justly ignored by such writers as John O'Connor. He's a mighty fine writer.

mitigate against.   This is a very interesting case.

The English language has two vaguely similar words—*mitigate* and *militate*. To *mitigate* means to soften and comes from the Latin verb *mitigare,* to make mild, soft or tender. To *militate against* means to work or fight against and comes from the Latin word *militare,* to serve as a soldier.

The trouble is that the American people constantly mix up the two words. They say and write *mitigate against* when they mean *militate against* and they simply don't use the word *militate* at all. For instance, the *New York Times Magazine*

(11/21/82) carried the following sentence: "He also wonders whether the leisure-time orientation of Los Angeles itself mitigates against excellence."

Twenty years ago the mistake would have been caught by the copyreader and if not, by the printer's proofreader. No longer. The *Times* is now riddled with misprints and mistakes of all kinds.

I looked up this common mixup or idiom in all the dictionaries. Not a single one of them mentions this extremely common usage. *Mitigate* means soften, *militate against* means work or fight against. That's it.

On the other hand, this "common mistake" is mentioned in virtually every book on English usage.

Modern American Usage by Wilson Follett says the two words are "a dangerous pair."

Fowler's *Modern English Usage* (2d ed.) says the mixup is a "curiously common malapropism."

Theodore Bernstein's *The Careful Writer* says the two words "are confused by many writers."

Bergen and Cornelia Evans's *Dictionary of Contemporary American Usage* says, "*Mitigate* is sometimes used for *militate.* This is simply an error."

William and Mary Morris's *Harper Dictionary of Contemporary Usage* says, "This pair . . . are [*sic*] sometimes confused."

And the *New York Times Manual of Style and Usage* says: "*mitigate, militate.* To *mitigate* means to ease or soften; to *militate* (with the preposition *against)* means to have weight or effect against."

How is it possible that the vast majority of the American population regularly falls into this trap? The answer is simple. Most Americans now living have been taught to read by the so-called look-and-say or whole-word system, which trains them to look at a word's first two letters and the context, and guess what it means. If they had been taught by phonics in first grade, they would focus their eyes on each succeeding letter and couldn't possibly confuse *militate* and *mitigate*. The third letter is an *l*, not a *t*, isn't it? But some 200 million Americans have never learned to see the *l*.

I'm afraid it's a lost battle. We might as well accept the fact that *mitigate against* is now an American idiom.

mitts.   If you're not a subscriber, you probably think of the *Wall Street Journal* as a deadly serious publication for business executives, written in unrelieved dull style.

Wrong. The *Wall Street Journal* is one of our best-written newspapers, with daily magazine-type features that are full of lively language.

The editorial page is deliberately brightened so that the busy, serious-minded businessman gets the maximum pleasure out of his daily reading stint. Slang is not forbidden on the *Journal*'s editorial page. On the contrary, it's encouraged.

An editorial called "Trapped in the FTC" (12/8/82) dealt with a controversial Federal Trade Commission rule on doctors' and dentists' fees. Opponents felt that the FTC was apt to meddle with purely medical questions. "But," the editorial said, "the FTC has said it is willing to keep its mitts off these questions."

Why did the writer use *mitts* instead of *hands?* He could just as well have written, "the FTC is willing to keep its hands off." But he didn't. He went out of his way to use *mitts,* knowing full well that in the sense of *hands* it's pure slang. Every single dictionary says so.

Using *mitts* in an editorial is sheer playfulness, a slight smiling wink, a tiny bit of amusement.

mom-and-pop. An article in the *Wall Street Journal* (1/17/83) dealt with a man who runs a tiny radio station in Vermont. The article quoted the 29-year-old bachelor as saying, "This is a real mom-and-pop operation, except I don't have the 'mom'—yet."

The expression *mom-and-pop store* has been around for some thirty years and is firmly entrenched in the dictionaries. Most of them call it "informal," although some accept it now as standard English.

Originally the kind of small store now called mom-and-pop was called a hole in the wall. Why was *hole in the wall* changed to *mom-and-pop?*

I was puzzled by this question until I read the definition of *mom-and-pop store* in *Webster's New World Dictionary*. It says, "a small retail business, typically family operated and now often franchised."

This seems to be a clue. *Hole in the wall* was a rather contemptuous term, not an expression the owner of the hole would use with pride. So some advertising genius, working for a large franchising company, invented *mom-and-pop.* Nice and cozy, a bit nostalgic, an urban parallel to the much-praised family farm. Note that it isn't *pop-and-mom.* It's *mom-and-pop,* with mom, the symbol of all homely virtues, in first place.

Maybe I'm all wrong and *mom-and-pop* is a genuine folk term. But I don't believe it.

To me, *mom-and-pop* sounds like a product of Madison Avenue.

mug's game. An editorial in the *Wall Street Journal* (1/20/83) referred to a Russian offer to move their missiles behind the Urals in exchange for the Europeans not deploying any missiles at all. This, the editorial said, "is a mug's game."

I looked up *mug's game* in the four major American desk dictionaries, but it wasn't there. The dictionaries cling to the conviction that *mug's game* is strictly British.

So I explored the *Oxford English Dictionary* and found, to my surprise, that *mug's game* has been a British slang word since the middle of the 19th century. Henry Mayhew in his famous classic *London Labour and the London Poor* (1861) wrote, "We sometimes have a greenhorn wants to go out pitching with us—a mug, we calls them." A *mug*, in this sense, was defined as "card-sharper's dupe."

In the *Supplement to the Oxford English Dictionary* I found that by the early 20th century *mug's game* had become a common metaphor: "a thankless task; a useless, foolish or unprofitable activity." It's still slang, but from a real card game where a sucker sits down with some cardsharps, a *mug's game* has developed into a phrase suitable for describing the give-and-take of international diplomacy.

murderee. *Murderee?* you say. Is there such a word?

There certainly is. I read it just yesterday (2/14/83) in *Newsweek*. Peter S. Prescott, in a book review, wrote, "The murder, when it finally comes, is a surprise: no one, I think, will guess the murderee, or the reason for his death."

I don't mean to say that Prescott invented the word. Not at all. It was apparently coined by the famous novelist D. H. Lawrence, who wrote in *Women in Love* (1920): "It takes two people to make a murder: a murderer and a murderee. And a murderee is a man who is murderable."

Once Lawrence had broken the ice, *murderee* quickly made a niche for itself in the language. The *Supplement to the*

Oxford English Dictionary lists eight more instances in print, including two quotes from Aldous Huxley, who used the word in two of his novels. In *After Many a Summer Dies the Swan* (1939) he wrote, "You're probably the sort of person who invites persecution. A bit of a murderee . . . as well as a scholar and a gentleman."

Not all dictionaries have yet welcomed the word *murderee*, but the unabridged *Webster's Third*, which prides itself on its all-inclusiveness, lists it and defines it as "the victim or intended victim of a murderer." This is not as elegant as D. H. Lawrence, but it'll do.

namby-pamby.   In a column about religion *(Newsweek,* 11/29/82) Meg Greenfield wrote about "the stock wartime chaplain of the movies, who, after a namby-pamby irrelevant existence up to the last reel, finally gets sore at the Japanese."

Namby-pamby, according to the *Random House Dictionary*, means "weakly sentimental, pretentious, or affected; insipid; lacking in character, directness, or moral or emotional strength; without firm methods or policy; weak or indecisive."

Quite a collection of undesirable character traits, you'll say. Where did the word come from? What is *namby?* What is *pamby?*

The solution of this linguistic puzzle goes back to the English literary wars of the 18th century. There was an elderly poet by name of Ambrose Philips, who wrote innocuous poetry, including rhymes for the little daughter of an earl. Another poet of the time, Henry Carey, who specialized in cruel satire, fell upon poor Philips and published a parody, which he called *Namby Pamby.* Then Alexander Pope got into the act and in poem after poem attacked Philips unmercifully.

The *Encyclopedia Britannica* (11th ed.) called Philips's poetry "simple and charming." I found two lines of his in the *Oxford Dictionary of Quotations:*

> *The flowers anew, returning seasons bring!*
> *But beauty faded has no second spring.*

Not exactly Shakespeare, but surely the poor man deserved better than to be enshrined in the English language as *Namby Pamby.*

newsburgers.   You won't find the word *newsburgers* in any dictionary. It was coined on Thursday, December 23, 1982, by Walter Goodman, TV critic of the *New York Times.*

Speaking of competitive advertising for nasal decongestants, paper products and hamburgers, he imagined some comparison advertising for anchormen. "Does Dan Rather serve up as meaty a newsburger as Frank Reynolds?"

The *Times* honored this fanciful word coinage by headlining the article

Weighing Anchors and Newsburgers

Splendid! They even refrained from putting *newsburgers* between quotation marks. There it was, the brand-new word, paraded proudly in big letters.

I don't think that *newsburgers* will make its way in the world and become part of the language. God knows, the news on TV nowadays is carefully prepared, prepackaged, served up to suit as exactly as possible the audience's taste—but *newsburgers* is still too intellectual a joke.

Anyway, if the occasion comes your way to coin a word, don't hesitate. *Newsburger* is not bad at all; see if you can do better.

newszak. Less than a month after introducing the word *newsburger* to the world, the *New York Times* (1/18/83) presented us with *newszak*. The headline read

"Entertainment Tonight," Television's "Newszak"

The article dealt with the new TV show "Entertainment Tonight," which had made a successful debut in New York a few days before.

"Entertainment Tonight," the article said, "used a news format for an essentially entertainment program, an amalgam that has been characterized in the industry as 'newszak.'"

Newszak, of course, rhymes with *Muzak.* As you probably know, that's a system of background music filling the air of restaurants, factories and stores. Some people like it, some people hate it, and some have adjusted their ears so that they don't hear it at all.

To call the TV news we're getting these days *newszak* seems to me a pretty ingenious joke. It says, "This isn't real news, it's a cooked-up medley of mild, bland entertainment— just as Muzak isn't real music but some sort of mildly pleasant noise."

I'm a sucker for this kind of clever wordplay. I suppose most people are. Remember that. Whatever you're writing, try to amuse your reader.

nickel-and-dime. The *Wall Street Journal* (2/4/83) wrote about Citibank setting up express lines for customers with at least $3,000 in their accounts. "Citibank," the *Journal* said, "has been a leader in seeking out high-deposit customers while discouraging the nickel-and-dime crowd."

I couldn't find *nickel-and-dime* in most of the ordinary dictionaries and had to chase it down in the *Second Barnhart*

Dictionary of New English (1980). Even there, I only found the verb "to nickel-and-dime," which means "to pay close attention to minor expenditures" or "to treat cheaply and stingily." *Nickel-and-dime* has been used in that sense since 1973.

However, the *Wall Street Journal,* using *nickel-and-dime* as an adjective, wasn't far off. A "nickel-and-dime crowd," I take it, is a bunch of customers with small deposits, always teetering on the edge of an overdraft, and "treated cheaply and stingily" by their bank.

The *Journal* asked a Texas banker for his comments on Citibank's express-line method. "I think it's sort of tacky," he said.

nifty.   *Nifty* is a nifty word.

It's the kind of word almost everybody knows and lots of people use often. It somehow *sounds* like what it means—smart, stylish, elegant, clever. It's a word of high and admiring approval.

Nifty goes back over a hundred years. There are oodles of quotes in all dictionaries, starting with the American classics Bret Harte and Mark Twain. It's a good old American word, to be used proudly and without the slightest apology.

And yet, the English teachers and dictionarymakers are prejudiced against it. "Slang," they say almost unanimously; don't you dare touch that word with a ten-foot pole. It was listed as slang in the predecessor of *Webster's Third, Webster's New International Dictionary, Second Edition* (1934) and it's still listed as slang in one of the major dictionaries, the second college edition of the *American Heritage Dictionary* (1982). Why? Because the English establishment of Victorian times didn't care for the word, and through sheer inertia the prejudice has lasted to this day.

Well, thank God, John O'Connor, the TV critic of the *New York Times,* seems to be impervious to such nonsensical attitudes toward language. On November 5, 1982, he called a new TV movie "a nifty little detective drama" and went on from there to praise it in several paragraphs, winding up by calling it "a very special television event."

I took my clue from that and watched the show that evening. It was nifty.

nincompoop.   This is neither an informal word nor a slang word. However, I thought I'd include it in this book, since it's so lighthearted and cheerful it deserves more frequent use.

Nincompoop goes back to 1676. The *Oxford English Dictionary* says it's of "obscure origin; probably only a fanciful formation."

That's delightful. How many languages can boast words of "fanciful formation" and keep them handy for over three hundred years? It's a little like *humongous*—someone thinks up a word that sounds humorous and meaningful and it takes root and stays in the language simply because people like it.

Nincompoop means a fool, blockhead, simpleton, ninny. I suppose it has held its place for so long because all those other words are more insulting and aggressive. *Nincompoop* is good-natured and gentle. Languages need words that express lesser degrees of undesirable traits. In a *New York Times* review of the TV movie *Witness for the Prosecution* (12/3/82) John J. O'Connor writes, "Ralph Richardson is splendid . . . when he's fulminating against the nincompoops of the world, not the least of whom is his aggressively attentive nurse." As you see, the use of the word *nincompoop* here is almost kindly.

Anyway, let's have more "fanciful formations" and use them more often.

nitty-gritty. In *The New Yorker* (1/24/83) the banker Felix Rohatyn was quoted describing his early experiences in corporate mergers. "That process," he said, "taught me a very important thing; namely, the nitty-gritty of what goes into making one of those deals."

Nitty-gritty is a recent slang word meaning the actual basic facts, elements, issues; the crux of the matter or problem; what is ultimately essential and true; the specific or practical details; the core. (I'm using the four major desk dictionaries.)

The word was formed as a rhyme on the word *gritty,* which refers to the coarse, hard surface of the rock bottom. The *Dictionary of American Slang* says it was first used by blacks.

Nitty-gritty is the kind of word that seems to us to sound exactly like what it means. I'm sure this is nothing but an illusion based on the fact that we've heard the word so often and know its meaning. I suppose it could just as well mean crocheting or a spiced bean dish or a children's game.

Anyway, it's an excellent word. Now that we've got it, it's indispensable.

no good. André Previn, the conductor, was quoted in *The New Yorker* (1/17/83) as saying, "When people ask me how long a particular piece [of music] is, I don't know. I'm no good at that."

What did he mean by "no good"? He clearly didn't mean *"not* good." If he was "not good" at estimating the time it takes to play a piece of music, he simply had little skill in performing that little job. In time, maybe he might learn to do better.

But if, as he said, he was *"no* good" at estimating time, that meant he had no such skill at all. That particular talent was lacking in his makeup. Due to this native flaw, he was totally unqualified to give an opinion.

The difference between *not good* and *no good* is enormous. *Not good* means less good than others, but perhaps improvable. *No good* means of no use, a total loss.

No-good is a slang term meaning, according to *Webster's Collegiate,* "having no worth, virtue, use, or chance of success." If you call someone a no-good so-and-so, you write him off as a worthy human being.

The letter *t* makes all the difference. No wonder foreigners have an awful time trying to learn English.

nope.   Can you use the slang word *nope* in writing? Of course you can. It's been done since 1888 many, many times. Perhaps the most literary example occurs in Ezra Pound's translation of the ancient Greek drama *Women of Trachis* by Sophocles. The line is "Nope, no proof without data."

I ran into *nope* in a splendidly written lead editorial in the *Wall Street Journal* (12/13/82). It was a serious, novel proposal for the Social Security problem, written in elegant and highly slangy style.

The editorial started this way: "We guessed that you didn't want to read one more word about the Social Security crisis. We don't either. But . . ."

Then followed a radical proposal to split Social Security into two parts—the worker's accumulated savings and welfare payments for the poor. This was described in some detail, with various alternatives.

The editorial ended, "Needless to say, no such solutions are being considered by any of the groups with the mandate to do something. Nope. They would rather huddle together, pushing and shoving one another. Well, okay. We are now out in front, and we dare them to follow."

So you see that *nope* has a place in modern writing. In the deliberately casual and aggressive framework of this editorial, the use of *nope* adds just the right touch.

normalcy. On December 22, 1982, the first artificial-heart patient, Dr. Barney Clark, got out of bed and took a few steps. A hospital spokesman said, "What we have seen . . . is what we should phrase as a return to normalcy."

The next day the *New York Times* reported that statement under the headline

Heart Patient Takes First Few Steps Nearer to Normality

Why did the *Times* correct the spokesman's language and change *normalcy* to *normality?* Because it still suffers from the "correct usage" syndrome and considers *normalcy* an incorrectly formed word.

This nonsense has been going on ever since 1920, when President Harding said, "America's present need is not heroics but healing, not nostrums but normalcy."

"No such word," cried the English teachers and "correct usage" experts. In 1929 one of them wrote, "If 'normalcy' is ever to become an accepted word it will presumably be because the late President Harding did not know any better."

Well, it did, despite the outcry. There are plenty of quotes using *normalcy* in the *Supplement to the Oxford English Dictionary.* In fact, there are several such quotes in the original

Oxford English Dictionary, going back to 1857, eight years before Harding was born.

My advice is, use *normalcy.* It's perfectly good English.

nothing . . . not.   This morning (12/30/82) I found a
double negative on the front page of the *New York Times.* The
sentence read:

"Nothing in the history of postwar Bulgaria points to an
appreciable measure of independence from the Soviet Union,
particularly not in foreign affairs."

This is a classic example of the famous double negative,
the kind that drives purists out of their minds. Theodore Bernstein, for instance, writes in *The Careful Writer:*

"DOUBLE NEGATIVES. Two classes of these constructions may
be noted. One is the common, gutter variety: 'Don't give me
no butter on my toast.' This is indisputable bad grammar and
vulgar talk. So if the kid says, 'I ain't got no pencil,' give him
one across the mouth and tell him to go out and steal a
pencil."

The other class of double negative, Bernstein explains, is
permitted—sentences like "Adultery is not infrequent among
this tribe."

This is the traditional position, vigorously defended by English teachers and editors. The fact is that the double negative—yes, the "gutter variety," as found in the *New York
Times*—is an extremely common idiom, used by everyone.
Turn on your TV and listen to policemen, eyewitnesses,
friends, neighbors, family members, disaster victims, criminals, passengers, pedestrians, shoppers, cabdrivers, strikers,
kids, Social Security recipients, welfare mothers, roommates,
marines, clerks, housewives, denture wearers, headache suf-
ferers, beer drinkers, cooks, appliance users, savers, sports

fans—the American people. Faced with a microphone, they'll instantly use a double negative.

The great grammarian Otto Jespersen, in his *Essentials of English Grammar,* calls the repeated negative "not illogical" and quotes approvingly Shakespeare and Jane Austen:

Shakespeare wrote: "Man delights not me; nor woman neither."

Jane Austen wrote: "I hope things are not so very bad with you neither."

Please don't misunderstand me. I'm not gloating over the *New York Times* using bad grammar. I'm simply pointing out that even the *Times* occasionally uses the normal American idiom.

not to worry.   I love England.

I've stayed there several times in my life for months at a time, I have family there, and I feel very much at home among the English people.

So whenever I find a typically English expression in my American newspaper, it gives me a warm feeling.

The other day (12/17/82) the *New York Times* critic John O'Connor wrote about an action-filled movie. "One begins to wonder," he said, "what the producers can come up with for a rousing finale. Not to worry. A couple of single-propeller double-wing planes are recruited, and Sam gets an opportunity, in midair, to jump from a plane onto a helicopter."

What prompted Mr. O'Connor to write "Not to worry" instead of the usual American "Don't worry" I don't know. Sheer playfulness, I suppose. Anyway, I was grateful for the little extra pleasure he gave me.

I looked up *not to worry* in my large collection of dictionaries and found that not a single American dictionary listed it.

Finally I tracked it down in the *Concise Oxford Dictionary* (6th ed. 1976), which says, "[colloq.] do not worry, there is no need to worry." It's all in lower case and most reassuring.

Just for the fun of it, I also looked up *cuppa.* Sure enough, the *Concise Oxford* lists it and defines it as a "cup of tea."

no way. The *New Republic*'s "Washington Diarist" (2/21/83) wrote about the Super Bowl football game: "Like everyone else I had planned to watch the game and drink beer with friends. But at the last minute I stiffened and attempted some work instead. No way. About halfway through the third quarter I gave in. . . ."

No way is now extremely common in speech but still quite rare in print. It's not listed yet in most dictionaries. The *Supplement to the Oxford English Dictionary* says it was first found in print in 1969 and means "it is impossible; it can't be done." *American Heritage Dictionary* (1982) says *no way* is "used to indicate definite negation."

No way (with the accent on *way*) is of course a different phrase from *noway* (one word, with the accent on *no*). That means the same as *nowise* or *not at all.*

At some point the American people felt that the simple word *no* wasn't enough. There had to be a more emphatic word with a rising accent, saying *no* defiantly, as a total rebuff. *No way* means "Absolutely not" or "Are you kidding?" or "What do you take me for?" or "Over my dead body."

Just as we have *ab-so-LOOT-ly* for an emphatic yes, so we have *no way* for an emphatic no. I guess it's here to stay.

no-win. U.S. Supreme Court Justice Harry Blackmun, in a *New York Times* interview (1/18/83), talked about how he wrote the decision that legalized abortion.

"I knew it was a no-win case," he said, "but I didn't ask for the assignment."

I looked up *no-win* in my dictionaries and found that most of them didn't list it. Only the very latest defined the word, which dates back to around 1960. *American Heritage* (1982) says, "incapable of affording victory or success."

Mankind had to get more than halfway through the 20th century until it arrived at the concept of *no-win*. We had to go through two world wars, the Korean War, the Vietnam War and the earlier Arab-Israeli wars until the uselessness of war produced a new word for the dictionaries.

No-win, to my mind, means compromise, wisdom, refraining from violence. It's a word that's never heard or quickly suppressed when war is near and tempers are hot. Witness all the wars that have been fought since the end of World War II.

nut.   Of the many slang synonyms for *crazy* person, *nut* is by far the most popular.

Nut used to be a word meaning "head." Next came the expression "off one's nut," and eventually this was shortened to *nut*, meaning a lunatic. Only forty years ago an insane asylum was commonly called a nuthouse. Nuts were simply crazy people, viewed without sympathy and ridiculed for their bizarre behavior.

We've come a long way. Insane asylums are now called psychiatric centers. Lunatics are diagnosed as schizophrenics or manic-depressives, and have a legal right to treatment. No one would call a patient in a mental hospital a nut.

Nut is now the word for mild eccentrics, lovable cranks or even sports fans. There are millions of nuts in our midst, and we talk and write about them with an indulgent smile.

Pauline Kael writes in *The New Yorker* (12/27/82) about Dustin Hoffman's role in *Tootsie:* "A stickler for the 'truth' in an actor's performance, he overcomplicates things. He's a nut—acting is his mania."

Vincent Canby (*New York Times,* 11/14/82) writes about the late French actor Jacques Tati as "Monsieur Hulot": "a gently foolish, pipe-smoking nut."

And John J. O'Connor (*New York Times,* 10/28/82) writes about a character in a TV comedy series: "a wonderfully off-center gal . . . played to nutty perfection."

The world would be a much duller place without all those nuts. God bless 'em.

off the wall.   In a long essay-review of a book on psychoanalysis in *The New Yorker* (1/24/83) I found this sentence: "The most off-the-wall of the analyst's interpretations may become true simply by having been stated with conviction."

This conjures up the picture of the patient lying on the couch pouring out his free-association thoughts and dreams, and the analyst interpreting what he hears by picking some ideas off the wall of his office. Apparently that's what the book under review says frequently happens.

Anyway, what exactly does *off the wall* mean? It means just what it sounds like. It's recent slang and the *Second Barnhart Dictionary of New English* says the expression comes from the handball or squash court. A ball that ricochets off the wall is unpredictable and seems to come out of nowhere.

It seems that we're always searching for new expressions that mean eccentric, unconventional, unpredictable. Ball games make good metaphors for that, and so we've had first *screwball* and then *flaky* and now *off the wall.*

OK.   So much has been written about the origin of the word *OK* that there's nothing to add. It's now the consensus that *OK* stands for "all correct." It was first used in 1839. In the following year there was a Democratic "OK club" supporting President Martin Van Buren, also known as "Old Kinderhook." (He was born in Kinderhook, N.Y.)

OK used to be slang, but most dictionaries now label it "informal." Actually, it has long been standard usage, not only in America and other English-speaking countries, but around the world. It's the most widely known and used English word.

As proof of its current high status, I'll quote William F. Buckley, the editor of *National Review.* Buckley is famous— or notorious—for his fancy vocabulary and generally high-toned language.

Recently, in the *New York Times Magazine* (1/2/83) he wrote an article about harpsichords. The article teemed with such words as *insouciance, numinous, desuetude, anachronized, detumescence* and *ineffable.* Toward the end he bemoaned the fact the harpsichord has lately fallen from public favor. "A harpsichord," he said, "will not sound out in the big standard auditoriums to which people go to hear music performed. OK. So the true believers listen to the harpsichord through records."

If this doesn't prove the current high standing of OK, let me quote from a *New York Times* interview (10/31/82) with Mr. and Mrs. Lou Eisenberg, who'd won $5 million a year before in the New York state lottery.

Mrs. Eisenberg, who'd suffered from cancer and whose health was still fragile, said, "We've had a lot of problems. I figured God said, 'OK, Bernice, you've had enough.'"

on the lam. If someone is *on the lam,* it means he's "in headlong flight, usually to escape punishment for a crime" (*Webster's New World Dictionary*). The phrase is pure underworld slang and has been so for at least a hundred years.

In 1886 a Pinkerton detective wrote in his memoirs: "After a pickpocket has secured the wallet he will utter the word 'lam!' This means to let the man go and to get out of the way as soon as possible."

There's no romance in sitting in jail, but there's plenty of romance in escaping. Newspaper writers are tickled to use the phrase whenever possible. Here are four examples from the *New York Times:*

A review of the film *Breathless* (11/21/82): "Mr. Gere plays . . . the punk who steals a car, kills a cop, and then goes on the lam with his girlfriend."

A review of a TV movie (12/17/82): "Sam is on the lam from a phony drug charge in Tucson."

A theater review (1/12/82): "Jessie is an overweight, shy loser whose husband has long ago left her and whose teen-age son is a criminal on the lam."

Headline on a front-page review in the *Book Review* (1/23/83):

Life on the Lam

Ah, they love it. They're against crime, but as soon as someone gets away with theft or murder, their hearts are with him and he turns into an instant Count of Monte Cristo.

ornery. Around 1830, the American people started to spell and pronounce the word *ordinary* as *ornery* and used it as a sort of euphemism for stubborn and unpleasant. Look up *ornery* in any dictionary and you'll find the definitions "lazy, shiftless, having a touchy disposition, inclined to be short-tempered, cantankerous, independent and individualistic, sometimes to the point of seeming eccentric, ugly in disposition, vile, coarse, of a mean-spirited nature, obstinate, base, having an irritable disposition."

What a collection of nasty traits! No wonder when a reviewer in the *New Republic* (8/3/82) wrote about the immense power of large corporate law firms, he said, "Only a rare shrewd judge, or an ornery one like David Edelstein, the judge in the IBM case, can equalize matters."

So don't shy away from the good old American word *ornery*. It's one of the worst things you can call a person, and yet it's a word fit to print about a respected federal judge.

outfit. Mostly, the word *outfit* means a set of clothes or equipment, and there's nothing especially interesting about that. But it also means "a group associated in an undertaking" or "a business engaged in a particular enterprise." Use of the word in that sense is labeled "informal" in the *Random House Dictionary.* Presumably it's not quite good enough for serious writing.

I disagree. *Outfit,* meaning a group of people, is a good old American word going back to 1879. It first meant a traveling party or a team of ranch hands, gradually broadening to cover any group of people bent on a common purpose. It's a Western, open-air word, with no trace of prestige or formality.

In the *New Republic* (10/18/82) Nicholas von Hoffman wrote about a racist book *Blacks and the Military,* published under the auspices of the Brookings Institution, a famous Washington think tank. He quoted from the book: "It is feared that an army composed of such a large proportion of blacks lacks legitimacy."

In the book's foreword, von Hoffman wrote, the president of Brookings said that views expressed were those of the authors and "should not be ascribed to his outfit."

Von Hoffman's choice of the word *outfit* was superb. An organization sponsoring racist literature doesn't deserve to be called by any more elegant term.

period.   "The real choice is between containing the Soviet Union in any and all of its global manifestations and not containing it, period" *(New York Times Magazine,* 3/7/83, p. 61).

Over the past fifty years or so, while nobody was looking, the English language has developed a brand-new colloquial interjection, called *period.* According to the *Supplement to the Oxford English Dictionary,* it is "added to a statement to emphasize a place where there is or should be a full stop, freq. *(colloq.)* with the implication 'and that is all there is to say about it,' 'and it is as simple as that.'"

Oddly enough, the English language philosophers latched on first to the new locution. In 1947 the journal *Mind* wrote, "The empirical evidence suggests the generalisation and supports it. If it does, it does. Period." In 1956 the philosopher J. L. Austin wrote, "It does not follow either that I panted whether 'I panted whether or not I ran' or that 'I panted' period." In 1977 the journal *Language* wrote: "If this is the view R got from 'On generative semantics,' he is illiterate, period."

Personally, I prefer the simple example given in *Webster's New World Dictionary:* "He hates cats, period!"

phony.   William Safire in the *New York Times* wrote about a speech by former Vice-President Mondale (11/4/82),

"He managed to strike a phony note of nonpartisanship without seeming oleaginous." The movie critic Vincent Canby wrote in the same paper (12/9/82), "Part of [the movie] takes place in the recognizable reality of Scranton, but the rest of it . . . is pure theater and thus looks more phony than necessary." *Newsweek* (12/13/82) wrote about government job programs, "They have often amounted to phony 'make-work' that furthered few long-range economic goals."

Phony is probably the second most common "informal" word we've got, right behind *OK.*

Once upon a time, back in the 19th century, *phony* referred to a brass ring sold as a gold one by a con man. (The word comes from the Irish *fainne,* which means "finger ring.")

But those days are long gone. Today phoniness has engulfed our whole life—in business, entertainment, politics, what-have-you. J. D. Salinger's *Catcher in the Rye* became a great classic because it described a universal experience—the realization that much of the world around us is phony and that the Emperor has no clothes on.

We yearn for the real thing behind the phony image and we're lucky if we can get a glimpse of it.

picky. The *Wall Street Journal* (2/2/83) had a story about the year-old California law that made forty-eight hours in jail mandatory for drunk drivers. The Los Angeles county jail got so overcrowded that they sent people to two nearby jails that charged $75 for an overnight stay. "The elite jails," the *Journal* wrote, "are picky about their prisoners and screen drunk drivers' records before accepting them."

Picky is listed as "informal" in the dictionaries. It means overly fastidious and exacting; extremely fussy and finicky, usually over trifles; choosy; excessively meticulous. As you see, the simple and expressive word *picky* says the same thing as a lot of highfalutin words.

Way back in the middle of the 19th century, *picky* was used mainly for "a picky eater." An 1867 dictionary defined *picky* as "of weak appetite."

Picky eaters we have still with us, but the world has gotten more complex. In 1977 the *Scientific American* wrote, "He was meticulous, even picky, about expense accounts."

Pickiness is the ultimate in choosiness. Said one official at a $75-a-day California jail: "We've had a few coming in that we didn't accept because they had bad attitudes. . . ." Picky indeed!

pinkie. On December 20, 1982, the great pianist Arthur Rubinstein died at the age of 95. The next day the *New York Times* ran an obit of almost one and a half pages, with four pictures, a separate article entitled "An Appreciation," and a vast amount of detailed information. The tone of the piece was set by the sentence "In the pantheon of 20th century pianists, Mr. Rubinstein's place is assured as one of the titans."

Way down in the article there was some information about Rubinstein's hands. "He would spread his spatulate fingers whose tips were calloused from years at the keyboard, to encompass the 12 notes from C to G—two more than normal. Moreover, his pinkies were nearly as long as his index fingers, and his elongated thumbs extended downward at an obtuse angle."

Did Rubinstein have pinkies? Is *pinkie* a proper word to use in a eulogy? I guess in 1982 it was. There's no longer any barrier that excludes light words from heavy discourse.

In 1808, an early dictionary contained the entry "*Pinkie*, the little finger; a term mostly used by children, or in talking to them." But that was almost two centuries ago. Even baby talk eventually grows up. Today, *pinkie* is standard English. Some dictionaries call it informal, but most of them don't.

Next time you hesitate to use an informal word, remember Rubinstein's solemnly eulogized pinkies.

pissed off.   This book is designed to teach you how to write better by using informal and slangy words. That doesn't mean, of course, that I recommend the use of so-called four-letter words. I don't consider them absolutely taboo, but I think if you want to use them in writing, you ought to have a good reason.

The *New Republic* (11/27/82) contained a book review of *The Boy Scout Handbook and Other Observations* by Paul Fussell, in which the author was quoted as describing himself as "a pissed-off infantryman, disguised as a literary and cultural commentator."

Fussell is a literary critic, widely praised for his elegant style. I think the phrase he used is apt and he probably chose it with deliberation.

I looked up *pissed off* in the major dictionaries. It's listed in the *Oxford English Dictionary, Webster's Third* and *Webster's Collegiate, Random House* and the *American Heritage Dictionary*. (Only *Webster's New World* among the majors omits four-letter words.) It means angry, disappointed, disgusted. The *Supplement to the Oxford English Dictionary* lists twelve quotes, including Norman Mailer, William Gaddis, Bernard Malamud, the respectable English journal the *Observer* and the widely read Canadian magazine *Saturday Night*. The first quote dates back to 1946.

Incidentally, the first quote of *piss* dates back to 1290.

pixilated. Pauline Kael, *The New Yorker*'s movie critic, loves to revive humorous old words. Having earlier used the fine old word *discombobulate,* she wrote in a review of an Italian movie (2/7/83) about a little girl: "Even the hops she takes, out of sheer pixilated excitement, are a bit higher than life."

Pixilated, believe it or not, is a variant form of the word *pixy-led.* A *pixy,* according to the *Oxford English Dictionary,* is "a supposed supernatural being akin to a fairy." *Pixy-led,* which has a separate entry with five quotes stretching from 1659 to 1895, means "led astray by pixies; lost; bewildered; confused."

Then there was the famous movie *Mr. Deeds Goes to Town* with Gary Cooper (1936) in which *pixilated* was explained this way: "The word *pixilated* is derived from the word *pixies,* meaning elves. They would say 'The pixies have got him,' as we nowadays would say a man is 'balmy.'"

Today, fifty years later, the common word is *flaky.* But why not use *pixilated* once in a while, just for a change? After all, *flaky,* if it reminds you of anything at all, reminds you of baseball; but *pixilated* reminds you of *A Midsummer Night's Dream.*

pizzazz. It isn't often that you find the word *pizzazz* applied to classical music, but it happened in the *New York Times Magazine* (11/21/82). In an article about the conductor Giulini, the author wrote, "This isn't the kind of overpowering, get-them-on-their-feet-and-cheering pizzazz of Georg Solti and the Chicago Symphony in its glory years in the mid-1970s."

Pizzazz is almost fifty years old—it was first found in print in 1937. Most dictionaries say its origin is unknown, but *Web-*

ster's New World says "probably echoic of exuberant cry." (I'm not sure this gets us much further.)

Back in 1937, the editor of the Harvard *Lampoon* said pizzazz was "an indefinable dynamic quality, the *je ne sais quoi* of function; as for instance, adding Scotch puts pizzazz into a drink."

Since then, *pizzazz* has been used innumerable times, with innumerable shades of meaning. Dictionaries have defined it as "liveliness, vitality, pep, showy quality, flashiness, energy, vigor, spirit, smartness, flash, style, sparkle, dash, flair, glamour, the quality of being exciting or attractive, flamboyance, zest, power, force, aggression, audacity."

Oh, I almost forgot: *Pizzazz* is also spelled *bezaz, bezazz, bizzazz, pazazz, pazzazz, pezazz, pizazz* and *pizzaz*. You take your pick.

pooch. What's the difference between a dog and a pooch?

A dog, according to *Webster's Collegiate,* is "a highly variable carnivorous domestic mammal (*Canis familiaris*)." A pooch, according to the same dictionary, is a "dog." No difference.

I went through all my dictionaries and got the same result. A pooch, by universal agreement, is the same as a dog. The origin of the word is unknown and it is generally labeled slang.

But the *Supplement to the Oxford English Dictionary* gave me some added clues. In the first place, it says that a pooch is usually a mongrel. In the second place, the quotes cited show that a pooch is normally a petted and beloved animal. In 1927, a story in *Collier's* magazine said, "At home, the trick pooch got all the attention, eating at the table with the family."

Newsweek (1/24/83) ran a story about the actress Estelle Winwood, who was about to celebrate her 100th birthday. The magazine said she lived in Los Angeles "with a housekeeper and her adored pooch, Lilly."

I think *Newsweek* used the word *pooch* quite properly. A dog is a dog, but a pooch is a beloved friend.

pooh-bah. In 1885 was the premiere of *The Mikado,* the immortal comic opera by Gilbert and Sullivan. Its famous characters included Nanki-Poo, Yum-Yum, Ko-Ko, the Lord High Executioner, and Pooh-Bah, the Lord High Everything Else. Pooh-Bah held all the high offices except that of Ko-Ko, and was immensely pompous and self-important.

Soon after *The Mikado* started on its triumphant hundred-year success, it was discovered that the word *pooh-bah* filled a gap in the English language. There were lots of people who held a whole slew of high offices and titles and were as pompous as all get-out.

The *Supplement to the Oxford English Dictionary* contains a long list of quotes documenting the use of the word *pooh-bah,* stretching all the way from 1888 to the present. One of them dates from 1962 and deals with the late dictator of Egypt, General Mohammed Naguib, and his "pooh-bah capacities as Prime Minister, Minister of War and Marine, Commander-in-Chief and Military Governor of Egypt."

I found *pooh-bah* in the *New York Times* (11/1/82) in a TV review by Walter Goodman. Writing about a show called "Six Great Ideas" with Mortimer Adler, he said, "Mortimer Adler is the pooh-bah of popularizers."

Adler, who was then 80 years old, was the editor of the fourteenth edition of the *Encyclopedia Britannica,* the author of the "Syntopicon," a compilation of 102 great ideas from "angel" to "world," the presiding genius of the Aspen Institute executive seminars, the originator of the Great Books college curriculum, and the author of many books, from *How to Read a Book* to *Aristotle for Everyone: Difficult Thought Made Easy.*

That's why Goodman called him a pooh-bah.

posh.   In a movie review in the *Nation* (12/18/82) the office of a society psychoanalyst is described as "exceedingly posh."

Where does *posh* come from? The unabridged *Webster's Third* says, "origin unknown." The unabridged *Random House* says, "?". *American Heritage* says, "Orig. unknown."

But the *Supplement to the Oxford English Dictionary* goes further. It says: "Of obscure origin. . . . The suggestion that this word is derived from the initials of 'port outward, starboard home,' referring to the more expensive side for accommodation on ships formerly traveling between England and India, is often put forward but lacks foundation."

For years I've been reading about this delightful etymology of *posh*. It conjures up the whole British Empire in all its Victorian glory, with traveling upper-class Englishmen and their families carefully sheltered from the inconvenience of the sun shining into their stateroom portholes. What a glorious, imperial word!

So now those skeptical scientific linguists want to take all the romance out of the word. "Lacks foundation," they say.

My advice is, forget about those doubting Thomases. Use *posh* wherever it fits, remembering the P&O steamers crossing the Indian Ocean, filled with well-dressed Englishmen, on the way to or from their Asian empire.

Like in the movies.

pro. In an article on the conductor André Previn, Helen Drees Ruttencutter wrote in *The New Yorker* (1/10/83): "He's a pro at bowing to the inevitable."

This is a nice example of the elegant *New Yorker* style. It's also a splendid use of the word *pro.* You see, *pro* has two meanings. One is the opposite of *amateur,* as in *golf pro, pro football,* and so on. The other means a person who is particularly good at something because he's done it many times before.

This experience usually comes from having worked on a job for pay. Doing a thing for the love of it is OK, but doing it for money produces a fine edge of expertise—the fruit of having done the thing many, many times when you were not in the mood. It's putting up with daily drudgery and resisting the temptation of idleness that makes for true professionalism.

In my own trade of writing, I greatly admire two sayings— one by Dr. Samuel Johnson and one by Mark Twain.

Dr. Samuel Johnson said, "No man but a blockhead ever wrote, except for money."

And Mark Twain said, "Write without pay until somebody offers pay. If nobody offers within three years the candidate may look upon this circumstance with the most implicit confidence as the sign that sawing wood is what he was intended for."

Wise men.

prof. Can you use the word *prof* in writing?

Webster's Collegiate says it's a shortening of *professor* and it's slang. No ifs or buts.

But that didn't stop the *Wall Street Journal* from using the word. On the contrary, they *like* to throw in a slang word or two in those articles they run every day for the entertainment of their serious, strictly business-oriented readers.

The other day (2/22/83) they ran an amusing piece about a "grammar hotline" that has been set up at York College in Queens, N.Y. A group of English teachers takes calls on questions of grammar, spelling and usage. "Reference books are kept on tables near the phones," the *Journal* reported, "but hotline profs don't hesitate to pull in experts on tough questions."

In the context of this fun item the short word *prof* was just right. It would have sounded wrong if the article had referred to "hotline professors." Once those English teachers started their dial-a-correction service, they forfeited their claim to academic dignity.

For all I know, they're wearing jeans and T-shirts while telling their callers about "correct English."

psych out.   Christopher Matthews, an assistant to the Speaker of the House, wrote in the *New Republic* (1/24/83): "Each morning . . . I am trying to psych out the current Reagan tactics. . . ."

I looked up *psych out* in my dictionaries. The phrase has an interesting history. At first it was used among psychologists and psychoanalysts, but didn't catch on with the public. Then, around 1970, *psych out* began to be widely used. Kate Millett wrote in 1974: "Mother's X-ray eyes met Celia once, had it all psyched out in three minutes." In 1978 Steven Brill wrote about the union leader Jimmy Hoffa: "Most others could never approach his ability to psych out the opposition's thinking so consistently."

What this means is that we've had psychoanalysis and professional psychology for almost a hundred years. We have tests and questionnaires, and personality inventories, and Rorschach tests, and deep psychoanalysis, and brief psycho-therapy, and dozens of scientific methods to figure out what's going on in a person's mind.

But people don't believe in such things. They have faith in intuition, instinct, indefinable ways of figuring out what other people are up to.

It may be a myth, but it's more firmly established than sci-entific psychology.

punch-drunk. There's a formal word *punch-drunk* and an informal word *punch-drunk.* The formal word, accord-ing to the unabridged *Random House Dictionary,* means "(esp. of a boxer) having cerebral concussion caused by re-peated blows to the head and consequently exhibiting un-steadiness of gait, hand tremors, slow muscular movement, hesitant speech, and dulled mentality."

The informal word *punch-drunk* has nothing to do with those alarming symptoms. It simply means befuddled or dazed.

The word *punch-drunk* dates back to the early 20th century; its metaphorical use started around 1950. By then, *punch-drunk* meant "groggy, dazed or dizzy for any reason; mentally or emotionally exhausted, esp. from a series of failures or personal misfortunes" (*Dictionary of American Slang*).

During the past thirty years *punch-drunk* has gotten less and less serious. Now it's just a temporary dazed feeling, nothing that a good night's sleep won't cure. After the 1983 federal budget came out, "TRB" in the *New Republic* (2/21/83) wrote, "Reporters are punch-drunk with all the sta-tistics they got from the White House last week."

It's just an expression, as they say.

pushy. William Safire's column (*New York Times,* 12/20/82) was entitled "Fighting for Life" and dealt with the case of Dr. Barney Clark, the first recipient of an artificial heart. It was a highly serious and thoughtful piece, discussing ultimate questions of life and death.

Safire is on the side of those who fight for life to the bitter end, asking the doctors to use all heroic measures available. He's against the currently fashionable view that "patients who refuse to resign themselves to the seemingly inevitable are pushy."

Pushy isn't exactly slang, but the dictionaries list it as "informal." They define it as "annoyingly aggressive, obnoxiously self-assertive, disagreeably forward." In other words, *pushy* is the kind of word that can't be defined by a single synonym and needs an elaborate definition to come even close to its meaning. It's a word people invented because it was needed.

The formal synonym for *pushy* is *ambitious.* That's an approving, positive word, which gives the person who pushes ahead a pat on the back.

The vast majority of people don't feel that way. They resent it if someone pushes ahead and shoves them aside while they're waiting in line.

quaintsy. Reviewing a new Italian movie in the *New Republic* (3/7/83) Stanley Kauffmann wrote, "Now comes still another style, the false naïve. *The Night of the Shooting Stars* wants to be a quaint epic told in peasant 'diction' with implications of tremendous themes. What we get is quaintsy hokum, transparently cagey."

Don't try to find the word *quaintsy* in any dictionary—you won't find it. Kauffmann made it up. And yet, in coining the word, he followed approved models, using the ending *-sy* to imply clearly that the movie wasn't quaint but only *fake* quaint. The makers of the movie tried for a genuine naïve style, but didn't make it.

Quaintsy is to *quaint* what *cutesy* is to *cute* and what *artsy-craftsy* is to *arty. Webster's New World Dictionary* says of *artsy-craftsy:* "having to do with arts and crafts; usually used in a disparaging sense to connote faddishness, dilettantism, superficiality, etc."

That's precisely what Kauffmann tried to say about the makers of that Italian movie. Using the word *quaintsy,* he brilliantly succeeded.

ratfink.   In her summary of the movie *The Towering Inferno,* Pauline Kael in *The New Yorker* (2/14/83) refers to "Richard Chamberlain as a ratfink electrical contractor."

What does *ratfink* mean? Let's begin with *rat.* A rat, aside from being a widely disliked rodent, is a police informer, a stoolie. This meaning has been traced back to the early 20th century. Naturally, anyone who rats on his friends is universally despised.

A *fink* is something like a rat, but in a labor setting. Back in 1892 there was the famous Homestead strike, which was broken with the help of Pinkerton private police, who acted as strikebreakers. The word *Pinkerton* was shortened to *Pink* and then changed to *fink.* A *fink* is therefore a hired scab— again a despicable, utterly contemptible human being.

Now we come to *ratfink.* The humorist Peter De Vries wrote in his novel *Let Me Count the Ways* (1965): "So cool and rat fink. What college did you go to? That made you so cultured and rat fink."

There must have been some unsung genius before De Vries

who thought of combining *rat* and *fink*. A *ratfink* clearly is a person who has sunk so low that among criminals he would be a stoolie and among union workers he would be a scab.

I can't think of any possible word that describes so aptly the ultimate of moral degradation. A *ratfink* is a born traitor. Put him into any surroundings and he'll instantly betray his friends.

And yet—the years pass and even the harshest slang word palls and loses its force. The 1982 *American Heritage Dictionary* defines *ratfink* as "a contemptible, obnoxious, or otherwise undesirable person."

What a comedown!

razzmatazz.   In the *New York Times* (10/30/82) its foreign correspondent R. W. Apple Jr. wrote about Spain's new elected leader Felipe Gonzalez. Apple described a rally in Guadalajara, which took place a few days before the election, at 11 P.M. "The atmosphere was intensely theatrical. Behind Mr. Gonzalez, who was bathed in spotlights, hung an immense banner with the party slogan 'For change.' . . . Loudspeakers . . . amplified the candidate's voice to earsplitting dimensions. And the whole shebang ended with the burst of clusters of aerial bombs."

In the next paragraph Apple referred to "the razzmatazz of the campaign." That slang word exactly fitted what was going on. According to the unabridged *Random House Dictionary*, *razzmatazz* means "showy and diverting but often meretricious activity."

I got curious about the history of the word. It's a fascinating story.

First there was the word *daze*, which goes back to the 13th century. It meant "to benumb and confuse the senses." By the

16th century the meaning had narrowed to "confuse the vision with excess of light or brilliance." To convey this sense of *daze* more sharply, it was made more vivid by changing it to *dazzle.*

By the late 19th century even *dazzle* didn't seem splashy enough to convey a really spectacular effect. So people changed *dazzle* to *razzle-dazzle.*

Finally, around 1950 *razzle-dazzle* was changed to *razzmatazz,* a word that originally meant early jazz music.

From *daze* to *razzmatazz* in seven hundred years. History gets noisier as it goes along.

ripoff.   What is a ripoff?

According to *Webster's New World Dictionary,* it's "a stealing, robbing, cheating, exploiting, etc." It used to be a strictly underworld slang term, but around 1970 it came to the surface and began to be used by law-abiding citizens.

The trouble with adopting underworld slang is that the words are apt to express the criminal viewpoint. If you're an ordinary person, you look at theft, fraud and robbery as crimes, and nothing can be said in their favor. But if you're a thief, robber, or con man, your activities seem to you defensible and even daring. You're an enemy of society and proud of it. If what you do is called a ripoff, it's glamorous rather than ugly, and you're something of an anti-Establishment hero.

The other day (1/17/83) the *Wall Street Journal* ran a long article on thefts and frauds of military equipment. It was headlined—naturally—

Pentagon's Big Empire Is Rife With Rip-Offs

The article was full of stories about a contractor who sold over 1,000 miles of defective nylon cord for use in parachutes;

workers who stole flight jackets, sleeping bags and even a $20,000 forklift; a computer company that stole $750,000 by falsifying records.

Such things are mean and nasty. Don't glamorize them by calling them ripoffs.

It just encourages 'em.

ruckus. The *New York Times* columnist Sydney Schanberg wrote (2/1/83) about Governor Kean of New Jersey, who disliked the American Empire furniture in the official governor's mansion, Drumthwacket. He said the pieces had "claws and hairy legs" and decided to heave them all out and buy a new set. There was such an outcry that, as Schanberg wrote, "the governor . . . decided to . . . end the ruckus. He announced that he and his family would never move into Drumthwacket."

What is a ruckus? And how does it differ from a rumpus?

I tried to sort out the history of the two words. *Rumpus* first appeared in print in 1764. The *Oxford English Dictionary* says it was "probably a fanciful formation" and defines it as "a riot, uproar, disturbance, row."

Next there was the Irish insurrection of 1798, which was commonly called a "ruction."

A hundred years passed and the two words merged into *ruckus,* which was also defined as "an uproar, disturbance, row." But there was now an addition: "a fuss, commotion."

The quotes in the *Supplement to the Oxford English Dictionary* show a progressive softening of the word *ruckus,* until it's now just verbal noise.

I checked the latest major dictionary, the *American Heritage Dictionary* (1982). It says that a *ruckus* is "a noisy disturbance; commotion." A *rumpus* is "a noisy clamor."

I would say that as of today a *ruckus* is just as nonviolent as a *rumpus,* but a *ruckus* is a few decibels louder.

scam.   *Scam* is a fairly recent slang word meaning a confidence game, a dishonest scheme, a swindle.

A few years ago there was a great national scandal involving several Congressmen, which became known under the name of Abscam. Suddenly the underworld word *scam* became a household word meaning any kind of dishonest scheme, whether run by criminals or by seemingly reputable businessmen.

The *New York Times* (10/18/82) carried an article in its "Editorial Notebook" which dealt with "the common practice of denying access to a checking account deposit days, or even weeks, after the checks are cleared." This, the article said, was "a petty scam."

A few days later (11/6/82), the *Times* again yielded to temptation and used the "forbidden" slang word. This time it appeared in an editorial referring casually to "welfare Cadillac owners and food stamp scammers whom the President . . . [is] so quick to denounce."

Scam is a classic instance of a word speedily moving up in the world. In 1966 it was strictly an underworld term that had to be defined and explained for the readers of the *Wall Street Journal:* "*Scam* originally was a carnival term meaning 'to fleece the public.'" By 1982 the august *New York Times* used the word routinely, whether writing of banks or welfare clients.

schlepper.   In the *New York Times Book Review* (1/3/83) Grace Glueck, a *Times* art critic, reviewed a new novel by Judith Krantz, *Mistral's Daughter*. She called the book "so stuffed with plot and buttery prose that it's—well, *fattening.*"

To prove her point, she summarized the plot. "Maggy, a beautiful French baggage with a mind of gold, leaves her home town of Tours for Paris, where she poses for Picasso, Chagall and Matisse . . . and falls in love with Mistral, at this point just another Montparnasse schlepper." And so on. (Mistral becomes enormously famous, of course.)

Why did Glueck use the Yiddish slang word *schlepper?* I suppose she had so much fun writing her review of Krantz's saga that at least one Yiddish slang word was needed to top it off.

What does *schlepper* mean? According to the *Supplement to the Oxford English Dictionary* it means "a person of little worth, a fool, a 'jerk,' a pauper, a beggar, a scrounger."

In other words, *schlepper* means something different from *schlemiel* (a "dope" or "drip"), a *schlimazel* (a "born loser"), or a *schmo* (a "fool").

All these words are kind. Yiddish must be the world's most compassionate language.

schlock. In her review of *Monsignor* (10/22/82) the *New York Times* movie critic Janet Maslin called it "the most extravagant piece of Hollywood junk since *Mommie Dearest,*" but noted that the producer, Frank Yablans, had also produced *The Other Side of Midnight,* "a schlock masterpiece."

What does *schlock* mean? It comes from Yiddish and means inferior, cheap, meretricious, of low quality or value, shoddy, defective, trash, junk. Between them, the dictionaries have used their meanest and shabbiest adjectives to define the word *schlock.*

And where did the Yiddish word *schlock* come from? Clearly, like most Yiddish words, it has a German root. However, the dictionaries are strangely divided on which German word *schlock* is related to. The vast majority connects *schlock* with German *schlag*, which means "to strike or blow." Only *Webster's New World* has what seems to me a much better idea. It says *schlock* has to do with German *schlacke*, which means dregs.

Knowing German, I'm all for the *schlacke* explanation. *Schlacke* not only means dregs, it also means refuse, dross, slag, sediment, scum, cinders, waste—any stuff left at the bottom and scraped from it.

That's what *schlock* is. It's the lowest of the low, sold to suckers for a fast buck.

schmaltz.   Reviewing a TV series "The Blue and the Gray," *Newsweek* (11/15/82) wrote: "Cut to a scene of undistilled schmaltz: the film's fictional Southern and Northern families gather for a euphoric wedding."

This is a typical use of the fine Yiddish slang word *schmaltz*, which originally meant chicken fat and now means, according to *Webster's Collegiate,* "sentimental or florid music or art."

Why is *schmaltz* always used to express contempt? It's the kind of people who ostentatiously don't watch TV who declare everything schmaltzy that caters to popular taste.

It didn't use to be so. Back in the 19th century even the most intellectual people read Dickens and listened to Strauss waltzes. And in the first half of the 20th century it wasn't shameful to enjoy a Shirley Temple movie. In 1951 Cornelia Otis Skinner could still write in *The New Yorker:* "What makes us weep is that happy combination of good theater and good pathos known as schmaltz."

In spite of all the sneering, schmaltz is what draws crowds and always will.

Anything totally without schmaltz closes on Saturday night.

schmooze. February 26, 1983, was the day when the word *schmooze* appeared in the *New York Times.* Mayor Koch was going on a trip to Israel and planned to visit with the peacekeeping U.S. Marines in Lebanon. Why? Columnist Sydney Schanberg explained: "The reason the Mayor wants to take the side trip to Lebanon, so he says, is to visit the peacekeeping United States Marines stationed there, so he can schmooze with them about the latest Con Edison hike and his appointment of Bess Myerson as Cultural Affairs Commissioner."

Schmooze is a Yiddish slang word meaning gossip or chatter. But it doesn't *just* mean that. It means gossip and chatter plus. It means idleness enjoyed to the hilt; it means prolonged intimacy; it means talking for the sake of talking. There is an art to true schmoozing, a ceremony of familiarity, a deeply felt extended pleasure.

In 1939 *The New Yorker* wrote: "Schmoozing in the garment district is more than just a lot of idle chatter. Schmoozing is a careful tradition dear to the hearts of everyone in New York's most thickly populated business section."

Schmoozing is the antidote to fast food.

screw up. Writing about a book on economics, Lester C. Thurow said in the *New York Review of Books* (3/3/83): "From [the author's] perspective, growth is the natural outcome of a competitive economy and something has to happen to screw it up, whether it takes the form of unions, cartels, tariffs, or selfish pressure groups, to name only a few."

Screw up, according to the dictionaries, means to botch, to bungle, to make a mess of. All dictionaries agree that *screw up* is slang. Where does it come from? The *Supplement to the Oxford English Dictionary* says: "This use may have originated as a euphemism for *to fuck up.*" The *Dictionary of American Slang* defines the word as "to ruin something due to blundering; to fuck up" and adds the warning label "taboo." It quotes J. D. Salinger's *Catcher in the Rye* (1951): "I never get really sexy . . . with a girl I don't like. . . . It really screws up my sex life something awful."

Why did Thurow use this taboo slang word with its clearly sexual overtones? Probably simply because he likes vivid, down-to-earth words and had no idea *screw up* meant anything more than botch.

Anyway, the *New York Review of Books* obviously doesn't give a damn whether its learned contributors use either four-letter words or words only a handful of people understand. Right next to Thurow's review was an article about a book on ancient Greece published in Paris (in French), which contained phrases like "the discovery of structural analysis as a heuristic instrument" and "the contrast between cunning nocturnal ephebe and stalwart daylight hoplite."

At that level of academic discourse the pop prejudice against slang and "incorrect English" is of no interest whatever. I'm sure the editors of the *New York Review of Books* let their scholarly contributors use whatever words they like.

sexy.   If you think the word *sexy* has been part of standard English for hundreds of years, you're wrong. It's quite new as these things go—a little over fifty years old. It was first spotted in 1928.

Of course it is used millions of times every day in reference to people. He or she is sexy, we say, meaning it as a highly complimentary description of a certain not quite describable set of features. "Miss Anderson," for instance, the *New York Times* (11/23/82) said, "came to television prominence as the sexy and bright secretary on the series 'WKRP in Cincinnati.'" If you've seen Miss Anderson, you don't need to be told what *sexy* means; if you haven't, you can easily figure it out.

Sexy, of course, is labeled "informal" in the dictionaries, which means "not to be used in formal writing."

Well, it certainly has been so used many, many times in the past fifty years. Nowadays we speak and write not only of sexy persons, but also of sexy novels and even of sexy cars.

shenanigans. Nobody is sure where *shenanigans* comes from, but *Webster's New World Dictionary* guesses that it comes from the Irish phrase *sionnachuighim*, which means "I play the fox." It's an informal word meaning nonsense, mischief, a treacherous or deceitful trick, or prankishness in general.

To my mind and ear, it's one of the loveliest and most melodious words in the language, with its Irish lilt and mischievous air.

I found the word in *Newsweek* (11/8/82) in a review of the movie *Monsignor,* whose contents were summarized as "orgies, violence and other nonsacramental shenanigans." Since the movie was characterized as "titillating schlock" and obviously not to be taken seriously, the cozy word *shenanigans* was probably quite appropriate to describe its wild doings.

It's a good word to have around. You don't want to get all solemn and excited about all the bad things that happen in this world. Take it easy and call them, with a half-smile, *shenanigans.*

shoo-in.   Every so often, before a political election, one of the candidates is considered certain to win and therefore called a "shoo-in."

For instance, that highly intellectual international journal *The Economist* (10/16/82) wrote: "Mr. Edward Koch, considered a shoo-in in New York's Democratic primary election . . . went on to lose."

The word *shoo-in* is at least fifty years old and very widely used. Too bad people pay no attention to word origins, otherwise they might have noted where the word comes from.

It comes straight out of the barnyard. *Shoo,* the verb, has been used since 1622 to drive away chickens by calling out "Shoo!" It is, according to the *Oxford English Dictionary,* "an instinctive exclamation" that has sprung to the lips of English farmers since 1483.

You notice that "shoo" is and was used to drive chickens *away,* whereas *shoo-in* means driving *into* office. How this 180-degree shift in direction came about is lost in the mists of history.

show biz.   Early in the 20th century people began to use the phrase *show business.* It meant the entertainment business—the theater, the movies, TV, radio—seen strictly as a moneymaking industry.

Then came *Variety,* the show business newspaper, with its

famous short-word headlines like "Stix Nix Hix Pix." Naturally, it called show business *show biz.*

By this detour the strictly-business word *show business*
was changed back into a word hinting at glitter and glamour.
Show biz means song and dance, drama, laughter and tears.
It emphatically *doesn't* mean the money-making side.

Reviewing a TV show about the armistice that ended World
War I, Walter Goodman in the *New York Times* (11/10/82)
wrote, "The producers resist using show-biz devices to obfus-
cate facts or to jazz up a dubious case."

In contrast, a review in *Newsweek* (1/24/82) of a TV series
about Winston Churchill said, "The producer couldn't resist
splashing on some show biz invention."

So now we have a division of labor between the two forms
of the word. *Show business* means the industry, but *show biz*
means entertaining make-believe.

shrink.   *Shrink* is a slang word meaning a psychiatrist.
It's a shortened form of *headshrinker,* an earlier slang word
making fun of psychiatrists trying to talk their patients' delu-
sions and hallucinations out of their heads.

Why do people have this contempt for psychiatrists? Maybe
they think that psychiatry still has to prove itself; maybe they
feel that psychotherapy is too long and too expensive. Who
knows? My guess is that the pill-dispensing school of modern
psychiatry enjoys better public relations and is less likely to
be saddled with the contemptuous label "shrink."

However, *shrink* has come up in the world and is now to be
found in the most respectable publications.

Recently, a *Newsweek* (11/22/82) movie review used the
word *shrink* twice as a simple synonym for *psychiatrist,* which
was used once. The headline read:

This Shrink for Hire

If *Newsweek* isn't elegant enough for you, consider the *New York Review of Books,* the most intellectual journal we've got. In a recent review (12/16/82) of a biography of Marie Bonaparte, an early leader of the psychoanalytic movement, the headline read:

The Shrink Princess

shtick.   Show business has a language all of its own, and much of it, not surprisingly, comes from Yiddish.

The word *shtick* is a prize example. I found it the other day (12/27/82) in *Time* magazine. A movie review said, "Audra Lindley . . . is a shtick figure—a garden-club gargoyle."

Yiddish words, like other foreign words, are used in English because they're untranslatable. *Shtick,* I found, is defined in the *American Heritage Dictionary* as follows: "*Slang.* 1. A characteristic attribute, talent, or trait. 2. A striking portion or detail. 3. The method of doing something. 4. An entertainment routine."

This adds up to nineteen words and four different, contradictory definitions—a mishmash of vagueness and confusion. But how else can you explain the word *shtick* to non-Jews who are not in show business? You can't: a shtick is a shtick is a shtick.

sincere.   In his column *(New York Times,* 2/22/83) Sydney Shanberg gave some tips on how to become a consultant: "It's a good idea to buy two or three new suits in a conservative style; your ties should be sincere."

What does *sincere* mean here? Obviously not, as usual, honest, true or genuine. On the contrary, it means faked or made up to appear ingenuous and appealing.

You won't find *sincere,* in this slang sense, listed in any ordinary dictionary, abridged or unabridged. There everything is quite genuine and aboveboard. But look up *sincere* in the *Dictionary of American Slang* by Wentworth and Flexner, and you find: "Having or deliberately creating a personality that is expertly charming and subtly ingratiating . . . in order to be accepted, liked, successful, or given preferred treatment."

Wentworth and Flexner say this slang use of the word goes back to around 1940. Anyway, it's still used by good writers like Schanberg. A "sincere tie" is highly descriptive.

I think this slang use of *sincere* in the sense of insincere is one of the triumphs of the English language.

sing.   The other day (12/16/82) William Safire, the *New York Times* columnist, wrote a sensational piece accusing the Russian leader Yuri Andropov of instigating the 1980 assassination attempt against the Pope. One sentence read: "When it became apparent to Mr. Agca [the assassin] that release was not imminent he began to sing about foreign connections he had refused to identify at his trial."

The word *sing,* as used here, is out-and-out slang. It's one of those words that are used all the time by criminals and by the police, but are rarely used in conversation, let alone in writing, by ordinary law-abiding citizens. Nevertheless, everybody knows what it means in this special sense—to confess to a crime and inform on others.

Used without fig-leaf quotation marks in the *New York Times, sing* is quite startling and apt to give a slight tingle to the regular middle-class readers of the paper when they read it over their toast and coffee or on the commuter train. But of course Safire, who surely has a free hand with what and how he writes, knows exactly what he is doing. The occasional underworld slang word makes for pleasantly spicy reading.

sitcom.   "Let My Sitcom Go" was the title of a *New York Times* editorial (3/7/83). The editorial dealt with TV show syndicated rights. There was no mention of sitcoms.

Where and when did the word *sitcom* slip into the English language? A quick check of the four major desk dictionaries shows the following: *Webster's New World Dictionary* (1972) does not list *sitcom.* It appears in *Webster's Collegiate* (1983). *Random House College* (1975) has "*sitcom. Informal. See situation comedy* [by shortening]." *American Heritage Dictionary* (1982) has "*sitcom* also *sit-com. Informal.* A situation comedy."

The *Barnhart Dictionary of New English Since 1963* (1973) lists *sitcom* with one example from *Time* (1970) and one from *The New Yorker* (1971). It defines *sitcom* as "a type of radio or television comedy series based on contrived situations built around a character or group of characters."

Now then. For one of our major desk dictionaries the word *sitcom* simply doesn't exist. Two of them grudgingly admit it as "informal." What does that mean? According to the rules of the "correct English" game, *sitcom* should not be used in writing at all or, if so, only furtively in casual, intimate letters or memos.

The fact that *sitcom* is used by everyone millions of times every day and thousands of times in serious business letters and reports supposedly has nothing to do with "correct English."

sleeper.   On November 10, 1982, ex-President Jimmy Carter gave an interview to the press *(New York Times,* 11/11/82). Among other things, he talked about the Democratic contenders for 1984. Mentioning Reubin Askew, he said he was "kind of a sleeper."

What did he mean by that? The slang word *sleeper* goes back to the 1930s and originally meant a cheap B movie that became an unexpected hit. Now it means anything or anyone who seemingly comes out of nowhere and becomes a success.

In late 1982 it seemed highly unlikely that Reubin Askew, the ex-governor of Florida, would become President of the United States. But stranger things have happened in our history. In fact, it might be said that we've had a government-by-sleeper for almost two hundred years.

The Founding Fathers, of course, had something entirely different in mind. They set up an ingenious and highly rational system to prevent an unknown or unqualified person from becoming President. There was the Electoral College, presumably composed of the nation's wisest men, picking the best man for President and the next-best man for Vice-President. In theory, that system was far superior to hereditary monarchy, which was a pure lottery, relying on whatever bundle of genes would become heir to the throne.

However, history almost instantly abandoned the carefully thought-out system of the Electoral College. Now we have parties and conventions and primaries and the snows of New Hampshire and TV debates and whatnot. Who will be the next President is wholly in the laps of the gods—the result of a long series of historical accidents.

This may or may not be better than hereditary monarchy, but it's far more entertaining.

slob.   On January 11, 1983, the *New York Times* ran an editorial on TV snobs. The evening before, millions of people had watched *Nicholas Nickleby* on the tube. This, the *Times* said, "created a problem for the true snobs among all us TV slobs."

As you see, the *Times* editorial writer didn't hesitate to declare himself a slob. The word *slob* had arrived in good standing on the editorial page of the *New York Times.*

It took a long time. *Slob* comes from the Irish word *slab,* which means mud. Around 1910, *slob* was, according to the *Dictionary of American Slang,* "a fat or ungainly person, esp. one of unattractive or untidy appearance." Gradually he rose to the position of "a hopelessly ineffectual person." By the thirties he'd become an "untalented, congenitally average person; any common man."

So, within a generation, the despised "fat slob" became the "poor slob," viewed with affection. Never mind the way he looks; he's just like the rest of us. Maybe he's sloppier than we like to think we are ourselves—but the difference doesn't really matter. He's what we all would be if we let ourselves go.

By now, *slob* is used with an undertone of envy. Ah, the freedom from convention. Inside all of us there's a slob who wants out.

smoothie.   One of the most intellectual magazines we have is the *New York Review of Books.* In a recent issue it dealt with the situation in Poland, Chinese education, Baudelaire, the civil war in El Salvador, the life of Thomas Mann, Social Security, art collecting, the class struggle in ancient Greece, the philosophy of Karl Popper, and a few other topics.

These highly diverse subjects are not necessarily discussed

in inaccessible language. The *New York Review of Books* doesn't shy away from the occasional slang word. For example (11/4/82): "Inexplicably, Bellamy seems to think that the most appropriate way to install [Tom] Wolfe's work on the top shelf of literature is to file away at those fangs and turn Wolfe into a soft-chomping smoothie."

A *smoothie,* in case you don't know, is "a man who has a winning, polished manner, esp. in dealing with women." The unabridged *Random House Dictionary* adds a helpful quote: "He's such a smoothie he could charm the stripes off a tiger."

So, if you feel the itch to use the word *smoothie,* go right ahead. You have the full authority of the *New York Review of Books* behind you.

snip-snip.   It isn't every day that you find the word *snip-snip* in the *New York Times.*

I spotted this rare item on January 26, 1983, the day after President Reagan made his State of the Union address.

Ten Republican cabinet members and thirty-five members of Congress taped their TV comments on the speech. "Two studios, no waiting," was the summary of the "snip-snip efficiency" with which it was done. "The politicians arrived like regular customers at the old barbershop, perusing Mr. Reagan's advance text as if it were *The Police Gazette,* and got into the chair, for a one-minute take."

A nice human-interest sidelight, showing the smooth publicity machinery of the Reagan administration.

As to *snip-snip,* I couldn't find the word in any dictionary. The *Times* reporter must have made it up on the spot, adding a nice touch to his description of the scene.

It's true that the unabridged *Webster's Third* and the *Oxford*

English Dictionary contain the word *snip-snap.* In fact, they contain the noun *snip-snap,* the verb *snip-snap,* the adjective *snip-snap* and the adverb *snip-snap,* plus the word *snip-snap-snorum,* which is a children's game. The basic meaning of the noun *snip-snap* is "a series of snips with shears."

The *Times* reporter was just one little vowel off. But then, of course, he was in a hurry to make the morning-paper dead-line. You can't really blame him for not using the traditional word and coining a brand-new one.

snooty.   In his *New York Times* column (12/26/82) Russell Baker wrote, "I'll force myself to watch the Miss America Pageant, the Academy Awards presentation and the Super Bowl on television. If the whole country is going to engage in these things, who am I to be snooty about them?"

Snooty, like *sniff, snuff, sneeze* and *snore,* has to do with the nose. As George Orwell wrote in *The Road to Wigan Pier,* "The real secret of class distinctions in the West—the real reason why a European of bourgeois upbringing . . . cannot without a hard effort think of a working man as his equal . . . is summed up in four frightful words which people nowadays are chary of uttering, but which were bandied about quite freely in my childhood. The words were: *The lower classes smell.*"

A snooty person is one who, literally or figuratively, turns up his nose at people he feels are below him. He or she can't stand their smell. The idea of equality is instantly lost as soon as the sense of smell is given priority. People who are brought up to be snooty will stay that way for life—unless they're educated to accept bad smells.

son of a bitch.   George Reedy, President Johnson's press secretary, was quoted in the *New Republic* (2/7/83) as saying about him, "He may have been a son of a bitch, but he was a colossal son of a bitch."

Son of a bitch is our classic insult. *Bitch,* in the sense of lewd woman, goes back to the year 1400. "You are a son of a bitch" was first printed in *Peter Simple* by Captain Marryat in 1834.

In the 150 years since, the force and sting of *son of a bitch* have greatly diminished. There's no longer any insult to anyone's mother—nor even any felt reference to her. And there isn't much of an insult to the son. The unabridged *Random House* dictionary defines *son of a bitch* simply as "1. a contemptible or thoroughly disagreeable person; scoundrel. 2. a disagreeable matter; chore. 3. an exclamation of impatience, irritation, astonishment, etc."

So you can now call someone a *son of a bitch* meaning hardly anything more than mild disapproval. You can also call an unpleasant job a *son of a bitch.* And you can use *son of a bitch* to mean something like "Really? What do you know!"

In short, the glamour of *son of a bitch* has long gone. If you want to get under someone's skin, think of something else.

soup-and-fish.   Andrew Porter, the music critic of *The New Yorker,* is a most erudite elderly gentleman with a prodigious memory that seems to stretch back over more than half a century. He's the kind of person who remembers with pleasure the performance of the second oboe when they did *Parsifal* at Bayreuth in 1922.

His reviews are miniature scholarly essays; no one in the world could be less slangy than Andrew Porter.

On October 4, 1982, he wrote about a concert staged by the Aston Magna Foundation, in which pieces by Handel, Vivaldi and Mozart were played "by a band of eighteenth-century size on eighteenth-century instruments or modern replicas of them."

Porter enjoyed himself greatly. "The pleasure and profit of hearing Mozart's music with timbres, balances, and phrasing that he would recognize scarcely need stressing today," he wrote.

But there was something that diminished Porter's full enjoyment. The players, instead of wearing 18th-century costumes to play their 18th-century instruments, had put on normal modern concert attire—"the old soup-and-fish," as Porter put it.

"Soup-and-fish"? I had read the phrase before, but had never figured out where it came from. Finally it dawned on me. Men's evening wear was so called because it used to be worn at formal dinners where the two first courses invariably were soup and fish. (I checked the dictionaries and sure enough, I was right.)

Porter's mild sally conjured up Victorian and Edwardian times, when the second attaché at the embassy in Constantinople was annoyed whenever he had to put on his dinner jacket to dine formally. A lost world.

sourpuss.   William Safire's column in the *New York Times* (2/24/83) dealt with President Reagan's habit of telling jokes. "Such remarks are ostensibly off the record," Safire wrote, "and anybody who grouses is a sourpuss."

Sourpuss is a slang word meaning "a habitually gloomy or sullen person." It's derived from the adjective *sour* and the noun *puss,* meaning face.

Or so you'd think. But language is never quite as simple as it seems. *Puss* is *not* just a word meaning face. It's an Irish dialect and slang word dating back to the 1890s, meaning exactly what we now mean by *sourpuss:* "a discontented, pouting mouth; a sour or ugly face." In 1978 the English newspaper *Guardian* wrote about David Frost's TV interview with ex-President Nixon: "On the air, Frost's pasty puss looked like Nixon's with the air let out of it."

In the United States the meaning of *puss* got weakened and it was used simply in the sense of face. So, some forty years ago, Americans began to call a *puss* a *sourpuss*. In 1947, the *Philadelphia Bulletin* wrote: "Out front will be the regular assortment of first-night sourpusses and professional runners-down."

Sourpuss surely says what it means. Twice.

so what?.   The other day (1/6/83) the *New York Times* book reviewer Christopher Lehmann-Haupt, a man not usually given to slangy language, used the expression *So what?*

He was writing about a new book by Bruno Bettelheim that said Freud's works had been mistranslated into English. The German word *Schaulust,* which means "pleasure in looking," had been translated as *scopophilia;* the German word *Fehlleistung,* which means "faulty achievement," had been made into *parapraxis,* and so on.

"So what?" asked Lehmann-Haupt. The whole thing was so abstruse that he had to break into slang to deal with it.

So what? is the classic American expression, according to *Webster's Collegiate,* "to belittle a point under discussion." Wentworth and Flexner's *Dictionary of American Slang* says it shows "lack of interest, or inability or refusal to comprehend the pertinence or enthusiasm generated by a speech, act, object, or idea."

So what? is the all-purpose conversation-stopper, argument-shrugger-offer, theory-dismisser, debate-ender. What difference does it make? Why bother with empty speculations? Let's get down to business and find out. Let's run it up the flagpole and see if anyone salutes. Will it play in Peoria? *So what?* is pragmatism as opposed to ideology.

spaced-out, spacey, spacy. In the 1960s, when the use of drugs first became common, a word appeared that described the state of mind of a user—*spaced out.* It described the indescribable feeling of being lifted out of reality and existing, free of earthly weight and cares, somewhere in outer space. That's the sense of the word *spaced-out* you'll find in dictionaries published in the 1970s. *Webster's New World* says, "under the influence of a drug, marijuana, etc."

But within a few years the meaning of *spaced-out* (or *spacey* or *spacy)* broadened. The 1982 *American Heritage Dictionary* says, "stupefied from or *as if* from a drug" and adds, "eccentric, off-beat." The *Second Barnhart Dictionary of New English* (1980) defines *spacy* or *spacey* as "dazed, stupefied, dreamy, unconventional or eccentric." *Time* wrote in 1976, "Her former boyfriends generally describe her as nutty, spacy, neurotic or dim."

My findings confirm the swift change in the meaning of the word. Reviewing a book by John Sack, Michiko Kakutani in the *New York Times* (1/31/83) wrote, "Mr. Sack can be glib and amusing in a stoned, spaced-out sort of way." And Pauline Kael in *The New Yorker* (12/27/82) said, "Julie has honey-colored hair and a friendly smile; she looks freshly created—just hatched, and pleasantly, warmly spacy."

Ah, some people have all the luck—they can be spacy without drugs.

splendiferous. Roger Angell wrote about "The Sporting Scene" in *The New Yorker* (11/29/82): "Nothing went right in the Bronx this year, starting with the club's winter decision not to renew the contract of Reggie Jackson, who moved along to the Angels and a splendiferous season of thirty-nine homers and a hundred runs batted in."

Splendiferous is a truly splendiferous word. It has a fascinating history. The *Oxford English Dictionary* lists it first as obsolete, with quotes dated between 1460 and 1546, and then stopping. In this early use, the dictionary says, the word meant "full of, abounding in, splendour."

Three hundred years after it died, *splendiferous* was revived, as a mild joke. In this second life the *Oxford English Dictionary* defines it as "remarkably fine; magnificent." The first cited appearance in print of the new-old word was in *Sam Slick in England* (1843) by the Nova Scotian humorist Thomas Haliburton: "A splendiferous white hoss, with long tail and flowin' mane."

Webster's New World Dictionary says that *splendiferous* is "a jocularly pretentious usage." But no other dictionary mentions this anymore. *Splendiferous* is now just another word for *splendid.* Too bad.

Anyway, thanks, Roger Angell, for using the word in all its glory.

stink. On November 1, 1982, Meg Greenfield, the *Newsweek* columnist, opened her column this way:

> JOHANNESBURG—*Every morning, when a South African gets up, he opens his paper and turns on the news to be told once again that the rest of the world thinks his country stinks.*

That's pretty strong language. You don't find this sort of thing very often in a respectable newsmagazine. But that doesn't mean that Greenfield is a poor writer. On the contrary, she is a very good writer, courageous enough to use the exactly right word where it's needed.

Not that *stink* is the most powerful insult she could have used. It has been getting weaker and weaker ever since 1225—yes, 1225—when someone chronicled it for the first time in that way. Nowadays, "it stinks" hardly means anything more than a mild statement that something is of poor quality. When you say, "That TV show last night stank," you probably mean that it was about 1 percent poorer than the regular run of shows.

It happens to all slangy metaphors. The number-one meaning of *bastard* is "illegitimate offspring." But by now, a *bastard* is just a person you disapprove of or even someone for whom you feel affection and pity. "The poor bastard," you say. "He hasn't had a decent meal for a week."

sucker.   A sucker is, first of all, a fish. It has been known by that name in North America since the 18th century. It has big protruding lips and feeds by sucking.

My unsupported guess is that suckers are easy to catch and that's why, in the middle of the 19th century, the word *sucker* was used to mean "a greenhorn, a simpleton," as the *Oxford English Dictionary* puts it. Current dictionaries list *sucker* as a slang word meaning "a person easily cheated or taken in."

You know about P. T. Barnum, who said, "There's a sucker born every minute," and the W. C. Fields movie called *Never Give a Sucker an Even Break.*

Lately, *sucker* has become a widely accepted standard word, used for serious discussions of serious matters. On the op-ed page of the *New York Times* (1/3/83) an article by Michael Kinsley, the editor of *Harper's,* discussed OPEC, the Organization of Petroleum Exporting Countries. "American banks," Kinsley wrote, "have done very nicely dancing OPEC's money back to OPEC's victims so the suckers can dance it back to OPEC once again, and so on even faster." A few days later (1/6/83), the *Wall Street Journal* ran an editorial, also about bankers. It wound up as follows: "Somewhere, we keep hoping, there must be a banker willing to say the emperor has no clothes, perhaps by declaring an outright default on a country loan. Until then, we really can't blame the Poles or the Romanians or the Brazilians for treating the whole bunch like suckers."

As you see, there are now greenhorns and simpletons manning the executive suites of international banks.

super.   The *New York Times* (12/25/82) had a story about Dorothy Smith, a first-grade teacher in the South Bronx, who had won a $5,000 public service award. Miss Smith was described as a dedicated and imaginative teacher with a thousand wonderful devices to help her "babies" learn. For instance, on her bulletin board, there's a section for papers marked Fantastic, Super, Terrific and Great.

Obviously, Miss Smith isn't aware of the fact that the adjective *super* is labeled "informal" in most dictionaries and is therefore frowned upon by purists. Not suitable for formal use—certainly not for official use with first-graders, whose tender minds might be polluted by this kind of slang.

Poor innocent Miss Smith. She tried to do her best. How would she know that vast numbers of words in daily use are on the proscribed list of the "correct usage" crowd? All she knows is how to teach little Ahmed, Jeffrey, Shamela, Isa,

Natasha, Brandon, Tamila, Arturo and Valerie the rudiments of reading and writing. If they can spell and read *super* and use it in a sentence, she's done a fine job.

The article said that Miss Smith also makes a special effort to teach her kids "not to bring street language into her classroom."

Super most certainly is *not* street language. It's excellent English.

switcheroo.   I found the slang word *switcheroo* in a theater review by Frank Rich in the *New York Times* (11/19/82). Writing about an English play by Wynyard Browne, he said, "The other sister is unlikely to quit her career to take Jenny's place. Or so it seems until Browne pulls a switcheroo in his third act."

Switcheroo is a playful slang word that has been around for some fifty years. In 1933 H. T. Webster wrote, "We'll pull a switcheroo. We'll use olives instead of cherries."

Since then *switcheroo* has had a splendid career. It's been used thousands of times to mean a switch, a reversal, a variation on an old joke or story.

Both the unabridged *Webster's Third* and the unabridged *Random House* dictionaries have elaborate definitions of *switcheroo. Random House,* for instance, says, *"Slang:* an unexpected or sudden change or reversal in attitude, character, position, action, etc. [*switcher* + *oo* suffix of appurtenance]."

However, when they put out the 1975 edition of their desk dictionary, the *Random House* people left out *switcheroo.* Why? They probably considered *switcheroo* too playful and had no faith that it was here to stay.

Boy, were they wrong.

tacky.   The word *tacky* has a fascinating history. Back in the 1880s it meant a scrubby, weedy horse. It was said that those inferior, "tacky" horses were the descendants of the wild horses of North Carolina and other Southern states.

Those were the days before the advent of the automobile. People were judged by the horses they owned, as today they're pigeonholed by the cars they drive. Poor Southern whites owned tacky horses and soon they themselves were called tacky. It meant shabby, not respectable, untidy, unrefined, seedy, dowdy.

Somehow the word survived a hundred years of history. Nobody now thinks of horses in connection with *tacky;* nor has the word now any connotations of the South or the social status of poor whites. *Tacky* now has a very distinct meaning—shabby, tasteless, and vulgar, all rolled into one.

Time (11/1/82) used the word in this specific sense. It reported that British newspapers wrote about a "royal tiff" between Prince Charles and his wife Diana. Diana was said to be "bored to tears." One tabloid reported, without proof, that Diana had bought over fifty ball gowns at $1,700 each and almost 200 dresses and suits at over $340 apiece.

Time called this "tacky reportage." They couldn't have picked a better adjective.

they, their, them.   "Did anyone, does anyone, perceive themselves as older than they actually are?"

How does this sentence strike you? It's from the *New York Times* (11/10/82), written by its staff member Enid Nemy. Is it grammatically right or wrong?

It may surprise you that three of the four major desk dictionaries (*Webster's Collegiate, Webster's New World,* and *American Heritage*) say the sentence is perfectly OK and there's nothing wrong with it. (The fourth dictionary, *Random House College,* considers it "nonstandard," that is, "not generally considered correct or preferred.")

Of course, everybody uses this idiom all the time.

The *Nation* (10/30/82) says, "Everybody, presumably, has their favorite and lasting impression of the President."

A newly employed ex-housewife says (*Wall Street Journal,* 12/8/82), "If employers can get someone younger than me, they'll take them first."

Senator Moynihan of New York says *(New York Times,* 12/4/82), "If someone wanted me to be their Vice President . . . I would say yes."

And so it goes. The fact is that English, unlike French, has no word that means "his or her." So, since 1526, we've been using *they, their,* and *them.*

tizzy.   What is a tizzy? According to the unabridged *Webster's Third,* it is "a highly excited and foolishly distracted or baffled state of mind esp. over a petty matter."

According to the unabridged *Random House Dictionary,* a tizzy is "a dither."

This left me in a baffled state of mind, so I looked up *dither.*

A dither, according to *Random House,* is "a state of flustered excitement or fear." It's a variant of *didder,* from the Middle English word *diddere;* compare *dodder.*

I compared *dodder.* It's a verb meaning "to shake, tremble, totter." Compare *dither, totter, teeter,* etc.

Having already compared *dither,* I next compared *totter.* It means "to shake or tremble."

I next compared *teeter.* It means "to move unsteadily." Compare Icelandic *titra,* German *zittern,* "to tremble, quiver."

Having done all this research in depth, I knew exactly what

was meant when the *New York Times* (12/6/82) reported that President Reagan's staff was "in a tizzy" when they heard that President Betancur of Colombia was planning to greet Reagan with a speech attacking the United States.

Obviously, the members of Reagan's entourage shook, trembled and quivered.

tony.   *Tony* is one of those words that start out with favorable connotations and wind up with a cynical, ironical undertone.

Back in the 1880s *tony* meant "in, of or representing the best society or latest fashion." There are several quotes in the *Oxford English Dictionary* that show this straightforward and wholly positive use.

During the 20th century the meaning of *tony* gradually changed. While most dictionaries still stick to "high-toned, luxurious, stylish, aristocratic," *Webster's New World* adds, "often ironic." And the *Dictionary of American Slang* adds, "snobbish."

In a book review in the *Nation* (1/29/83) the writer says, "The family lived on Manhattan's tony Upper East Side."

Am I oversensitive or do I hear a slightly disparaging note in this labeling of the address? *Tony* seems to be used nowadays only by those who look at wealth and luxury from the other side of society. Even real estate agents would hardly use the word *tony* in their ads and listings.

toot.   Winding up a rave review of the movie *Tootsie*, Vincent Canby of the *New York Times* wrote (12/17/82), "It's a toot, a lark, a month in the country."

The word *toot* isn't used much nowadays but of course it was a nice play on words to use it to describe the movie *Tootsie*. It means a spree, a binge or, as the unabridged *Webster's Third* puts it, "an act or period of unrestrained indulgence in some feeling or activity."

Nobody knows exactly where this use of the word comes from. There's the verb *toot*, which means blowing a horn, but the link between that and a binge or spree isn't clear. However, making merry noises on a horn and having a good time fits together somehow. It's something of an old-fashioned word, and who knows, back in the 19th century horn-blowing was more common in connection with noisy parties and gaiety.

Anyway, it was a nice touch to call *Tootsie* a toot. That's the kind of reviewing that sells tickets.

traipse. An article in the *New Republic* (9/6/82) said: "He was able to confirm [the story] by enterprising telephone calls from his office, not by traipsing down corridors in the Executive Office."

I love the word *traipse*. It means to walk aimlessly or idly, tramp about, gad, wander. It goes back to 1600 or so. Swift wrote in his *Journal to Stella* on March 2, 1711: "I was traipsing today with your Mr. Sterne." Alexander Pope wrote in *The Dunciad* (1728): "See next two slipshod Muses traipse along."

It's something of a puzzle that *traipse*, after almost four hundred years of respectable literary use, is still an "informal" word, held in disdain by the dictionaries. Maybe it's the meaning of the word, the unbusinesslike meandering and strolling around, looked down upon by our puritan work ethic.

But then, *strolling* or *meandering* are standard words, held in high esteem. So I guess it must be the funny *ps* sound. Words with *ps* are not taken seriously. Think of *oops,* think of *whoops,* think of *tipsy,* think of *popsy.*

Either I'm quite wrong or I've made a tiny contribution to linguistics.

trendy.   *Trendy* is a fairly recent import from England, now getting more and more common in the United States. It means fashionable, stylish, faddish.

The trouble with *trendy* is that its meaning depends on where you sit. Take, for instance, this recent sentence from the *Nation* (11/6/82): "If trendy elements of the liberal establishment don't support the [nuclear] freeze movement that is too bad. . . ."

What does the *Nation* mean by "trendy elements"? The *Washington Post* and the *New York Times,* both of which came out against the nuclear freeze amendment. Those two papers, in turn, might call the *Nation* trendy.

Or take a book review in *Newsweek* (6/7/82). A female fictional detective is described as "32, divorced, eschews the trendy, favors the slob school of fashion, runs."

The trendy that she eschews seems to be the well-groomed and unathletic. But aren't her sloppy way of dressing and her running equally trendy?

Anyway, why is *trendy* always used to downgrade people? There are lots of trends, pointing in various directions. Some people follow one and some another.

Trendy, as far as I can see, means following a trend you don't like.

tummy.   The *New York Times* (2/9/83) reported that at the annual Toy Fair the makers of "Care Bears" put out a release that said, "Each bear captures and expresses a human emotion and personality which is illustrated by a symbol on its tummy."

Tummy is not a word that's held in high regard by dictionarymakers. *Webster's New World* says it's "a child's word." *Random House* says it's "baby-talk for stomach." And the *Dictionary of Contemporary American Usage* by Bergen and Cornelia Evans says, *"Tummy* is simply disgusting when used by anyone over the age of four."

In spite of this prejudice by the English-teaching establishment, *tummy* has a respectable history, going back to 1868, when W. S. Gilbert wrote in the *Bab Ballads,* "Why should I hesitate to own, That pain was in his little tummy?" And in 1952, an Associated Press report said, "An elephant died of an outsize tummyache at London Airport."

There's a sort of macho attitude among the predominantly male grammar-and-usage pundits. They just don't *like* words mainly used by women and children.

But things are changing. Like *hanky* and *pinkie, tummy* is coming into its own. The 1982 *American Heritage Dictionary* says, unsnootily, *"tummy. Informal.* The stomach."

unbamboozle.   Recently (1/22/83) Christopher Hitchens started his column in the *Nation* with this sentence: "It was once said of, I think, Herbert Hoover that he was a hard man to bamboozle but, once bamboozled, a *very* hard man to unbamboozle."

I greatly enjoyed this joke. It hinges, of course, on the delightful word *unbamboozle.* Whoever used it first deserves a special award for enriching the English language.

Here we are, being the targets and victims of bamboozling all day long. Our whole environment—newspapers, magazines, radio, TV, billboards and skywriting—is designed to bamboozle us. Buy this, rent that, watch this TV show, go to that movie, drink this, smoke that, and so on endlessly. How much of it is bamboozling? You might as well ask, How much of this is the exact, 100 percent accurate truth? Very, very little, as all of us know. Like fish in water, we swim in a sea of untruths, half-truths and near-truths, resigned to the fact that being bamboozled is a fact of life.

Oh, for the unbamboozled life. What would it be like to breathe the air in a country where everything you see and hear is fully reliable?

I'm afraid we'll never know.

underwhelm.   Seymour Rosen, managing director of the Pittsburgh Orchestra, was quoted in *The New Yorker* (1/10/83): "When [André Previn] rehearsed The Pittsburgh [for the first time], my reaction was very much the same as the orchestra's—underwhelmed."

Underwhelm is one of my favorite words in the English language. Or is it in the English language? It was coined only very recently and most dictionaries don't list it.

But that's just the point. One day in the 1960s some witty, playful person noticed that there's no word that's the opposite of *overwhelmed.* The *Barnhart Dictionary of New English Since 1963* quotes an article in *Time* magazine (1968): "Rockefeller's long, prepared speeches in more formal settings often underwhelm his audience."

Did the *Time* writer invent the word? Or was he following in someone else's footsteps? No matter: *underwhelm* is a splendid word. It says in just the right ironic tone of voice that the speech, performance or whatever, far from overwhelming the audience, left them cold and unmoved.

I have two dictionaries that were published in 1982. One is the *American Heritage Dictionary*. It lists *underwhelm* as if it had always been a part of the language, and defines it soberly: "To fail to excite, stimulate or impress."

The other 1982 dictionary, the *New York Times Everyday Dictionary*, lists *underwhelm* too, and defines it as "fail to overwhelm."

They didn't get the joke.

unfetching. *Newsweek* (1/11/83) reported the discovery of a new subatomic particle. "They have been given the unfetching name of 'intermediate vector bosons,'" the magazine said.

I love words like *unfetching.* It isn't a word you read or hear every day, and most dictionaries skip it. But I managed to track it down below the line in a list of hundreds of *un-* words in the unabridged *Random House Dictionary. Newsweek* didn't exactly invent the word, but it dug deep to find it.

It was well worth finding. *Fetching* means "very attractive; charming," so *unfetching* means "not very attractive or charming." To apply the adjective to the name "intermediate vector bosons" is nice and amusing.

When you write, explore the possibilities of *un-* words. The *Random House Dictionary* lists a vast number, from *unabashable* to *unyachtsmanlike*. There are also *unfascinating, undelicious, unshrewd, unmonumental, unbrilliant,* and *unadorable.* Or you may invent a new one. Let me see now— how about *unsuperb?*

You take it from there. Find a highly potent adjective, turn it on its head by putting *un-* in front of it, and you've given your reader a little extra amusement.

Don't be unenterprising about your language.

unflappable.   To *flap*, in one of its meanings, means "to swing or sway about loosely; to flutter or oscillate as when moved by the wind." The word *flap* in that sense goes back to the 16th century. It took the British until the 1960s, when faced with the wholly unruffled behavior of Prime Minister Harold Macmillan, to invent the word *unflappable* to characterize him. This delightful invention has been around ever since, describing a politician who's fazed by nothing—at least visibly. The *Random House College Dictionary,* not gifted with much of a sense of humor, stolidly defines *unflappable* as *"Slang:* not easily upset or confused esp. in a crisis; imperturbable."

The *New York Times,* slang or no slang, uses the word when it fits. During the 1982 senatorial election, Congresswoman Millicent Fenwick, a charming pipe-smoking grandmother, was faced by Frank R. Lautenberg, a middle-aged businessman with no charm, no eccentricities, no visible TV attractions. How did he win? By being deliberately boring, but sticking to his views of the issues and appearing like the Rock of Gibraltar. "The candidate," the *Times* wrote, "wore nothing but blue suits, pin-striped or solid—appeared unflappable at all times, and spoke logically, if without passion."

He won the race.

uppity.   In *The New Yorker* (1/24/83) Janet Kramer wrote about the French people and their "uppity xenophobia of wallflowers at a superpowers ball."

That's *New Yorker* style in all its glory. Take the $10 word *xenophobia,* which means "an unreasonable fear or hatred of foreigners or strangers." It's a trait often ascribed to people living far from civilization. The *Oxford English Dictionary* has a quote about xenophobia among Afghans.

But of course that connotation of xenophobia doesn't fit the French. So Janet Kramer, writing about the special French kind of xenophobia, called it "uppity."

Uppity is an informal word meaning haughty or snobbish. The word is only about thirty years old and is listed in the *Dictionary of American Slang.*

The adjective *uppity* distinguishes the French kind of xenophobia from the Afghan kind.

If you can write a phrase like "uppity xenophobia," you can write.

uptight. Diane Sawyer, the co-anchorwoman of the "CBS Morning News," wakes up every weekday at 1:30 A.M., exercises for fifteen minutes, races through the *New York Times,* and does some last-minute homework. Then she takes a taxi and gets to the CBS studio by 3:30 A.M., scans wire copy, jots down some notes. At 7 A.M. she says "Good morning to all of you" to millions of viewers.

Newsweek (3/14/83) described this grueling schedule. The magazine said that when Sawyer debuted on her job in the fall of 1981, "she was visibly uptight about her lack of training as an anchor [and] projected all the warmth of a splash of ice water."

Uptight obviously described her condition exactly. It's a slang word, dating back some ten or fifteen years, meaning keyed up like a watch spring, tense, anxious, hung up, nervous, jittery, very uneasy or apprehensive.

Well, how would *you* feel if you had to smilingly greet millions of people at seven o'clock in the morning?

vroom-vroom. Here's a sentence from Meg Greenfield's column in *Newsweek* (9/20/82): "The guy with the penchant for diamond pinkie rings or six-course dinners or exotic sex or vroom-vroom cars . . . will cut corners to acquire these things."

Vroom-vroom? I looked through all my dictionaries but was only partially successful. The double *vroom-vroom* simply isn't listed anywhere. Single *vrooms* are listed in *Webster's Collegiate, Webster's New World,* the *New York Times Everyday Dictionary,* the *Dictionary of American Slang,* and the *Barnhart Dictionary of New English Since 1963.* The simplest definition is that of the *New York Times Everyday Dictionary:* "the sound of a speeding sports car."

Why did Greenfield use *vroom-vroom cars* instead of *sports cars?* Obviously because it's vastly more fun to write. A word that imitates the sound of what you're writing about is always preferable to one that's silent—just lies there (or lays there) on the page.

Moral: Use our English noisemakers—*vroom-vroom, pfft, brrr, ouch, ooh, ugh, uh-uh,* and so on. Sprinkle them on the page.

was. In the fall of 1982 Senator Edward Kennedy withdrew from the 1984 presidential race. He said it was a family decision. "If I was to make a political decision," he said, "it would be a different announcement today."

In his Sunday language column in the *New York Times* (1/9/83) William Safire took Kennedy to task for using bad grammar. "When you are posing a hypothesis contrary to fact," he wrote, "you must use the subjunctive." Therefore, Kennedy should have said, "If I *were* to make a political decision . . ."

Safire was some three hundred years out of date. The use of *was* in such contrary-to-fact conditional clauses goes back to 1684, when John Bunyan wrote, "As if one was awake."

Essentials of English Grammar by Otto Jespersen says, "Since the 17th century we see an increasing tendency to say *I wish he was* . . . , *as if he was* . . . , *if he was* . . . instead of the earlier *were.*"

The *Dictionary of Contemporary American Usage* by Bergen and Cornelia Evans says, "*Was* may be used in . . . *I wish I was wonderful, suppose it was true,* and *if I was living in a desert.* . . . *Was* has been used as a past subjunctive in literary English for more than three hundred years and is the preferred form today."

I think if I was William Safire, I'd lay off that ancient usage.

weirdo.   Meg Greenfield, the *Newsweek* columnist, has the true gift of writing. On a good day, in front of her typewriter, she's unbeatable. Listen to her in full flight (7/26/82): "Everyone knew the Iraqis would beat the Iranians because they were well-armed and -trained martial-looking third-worlders against a bunch of ululating weirdos carrying pictures of the Ayatollah Khomeini."

What's a *weirdo?* According to the tight-lipped *American Heritage Dictionary,* he, she or it is "an unusually strange person, thing or event." The *Dictionary of American Slang* adds: "The word applies equally well to introverts, geniuses, homosexuals, abstract painters and their products, bird watchers, etc., and may be applied to any nonconformist."

Weirdo became popular around 1950. At first the word was *weirdie,* but some ten or twenty years ago it was changed to *weirdo.* Why? Nobody knows, except that the ending *-o* is now generally used to express contempt. Listen to a few *-o* words—*bozo, dipso, fatso, nympho, pinko, psycho, schizo, stinko, wacko, wino, wrongo.* While nobody was looking, the American people invented a new, widely used ending.

Anyway, a weirdo is almost a creep. Or creepo.

whee! In *Newsweek* (2/7/83) Gene Lyons reviewed a book on nuclear war. The author had interviewed a high Pentagon official who explained how everybody could survive such a war: "Dig a hole, cover it with a couple of doors and then throw three feet of dirt on top. . . . if there are enough shovels to go around everybody's going to make it."

To which Lyons added a single word: "Whee!"

I think the word *whee!* (including the exclamation point) was the only even remotely adequate comment on that staggering, unbelievably stupid pronouncement. There are situations in writing when all words fail and only the most elementary exclamation will do.

Don't shy away from using exclamations in your writing. Write *whee, wow, gosh, gee, oh boy, holy mackerel*—whatever springs to your lips. And use exclamation points whenever they're called for. How else can you express strong emotion?

People think that all prepared or formal writing must be monotonous, detached, studiously unemphatic. Why? If you're writing about something exciting, show your excitement. Raise your voice.

who. Since the early 1300s English-speaking people have expressed a dislike for the word *whom* and have used *who* where strict grammar would call for *whom*. Marlowe wrote, "Who have ye there, my lordes?" Shakespeare wrote, "Who didst thou leave to tend his Majesty?" Sheridan wrote, "Who can he take after?" George Eliot wrote, "But he didn't know who he was talking to."

The trend is still as strong as ever. In the *New York Review of Books* I found recently (12/16/82): "Being influenced is partly a question of who you choose to be influenced by."

Common and accepted as this usage is, it still drives purists utterly mad. Here, for example, is an outbreak from John Simon, the author of *Paradigms Lost* (1980): "Why should we lose this useful distinction? Just because a million or ten million or a billion people less educated than we are cannot master the difference? Surely it behooves us to try to educate the ignorant up to our level rather than to stultify ourselves down to theirs."

The truth is that Mr. Simon, who thinks it's his mission to educate a billion others, doesn't know a thing about scientific linguistics. The great grammarian Otto Jespersen wrote (*Essentials of English Grammar*, 1933), "The form *who* . . . is now practically the only form used in colloquial speech. . . . Grammarians have been so severe in blaming this that now many people feel proud when they remember writing *whom* and even try to use that form in speech."

Don't force yourself to use *whom*. Use *who*.

whodunit.   On February 14, 1983, *Time* magazine reviewed Julian Symons's new mystery *The Detling Secret*. It called it "a novel molded into the shape of the classical whodunit."

Whodunit is obviously the kind of word that was playfully coined by a brilliant mind. There are at least four contenders for the honor. First there was Sime Silverman, a former editor of *Variety* magazine who was supposed to have coined the word in 1936. This claim was supported by his successor

Abel Green. Next there was another *Variety* editor, Wolfe Kaufman, who said *he* coined the word in 1935. Next, a researcher came up with the story that *whodunit* was an invention of the English humorist P. G. Wodehouse around 1930. Finally, *Funk & Wagnall's Standard College Dictionary* (1963) attributed the word to Donald Gordon, who used it in 1930 in the magazine *American News of Books.*

Whoever it was did a splendid job. Of course, the exact phrase would have been "who did it," but who cares? *Whodunit* sounds much better and trips easily off the tongue.

But the stolid unabridged *Webster's Third* has no truck with such considerations. It lists *whodunit* and adds, with a sharp rap on the knuckles: "From the substandard expression *who done it."*

whom.   *Whom,* oddly enough, is still alive and used commonly in certain places where the "correct" grammatical form would be *who.*

For instance, in a *New York Times Magazine* article on conductors (11/28/82) the *Times'* chief music critic, Donald Henahan, writes: "At the source of it all . . . we find the man whom musical historians have decided was the 'first conductor': Jean Baptiste Lully."

This *whom,* by the strict rules of grammar, should have been *who.* But popular idiom, in its unfathomable perversity, insists on this kind of *whom.* It's been around since 1467. The *Oxford English Dictionary,* around 1920 or so, calls this usage "ungrammatical" and "erroneous," but gives us a dozen or more highly reputable quotes. Izaak Walton wrote in *The Compleat Angler* (1653): "Comparing the humble epistles of S. Peter, S. James and S. John, whom we know were Fishers, with the glorious language of S. Paul, who we know was not."

Dickens wrote in *The Pickwick Papers* (1837): "A strange un-earthly figure, whom Gabriel felt at once was no being of this world."

What would the English language be without its lovable quirks?

whoppingest. *Newsweek* columnist George Will wrote (1/17/83): "[When President Reagan was governor of California] he raised income taxes and sales, liquor, ciga-rette, bank, insurance and corporation taxes—the whop-pingest increase in his state's history."

Whoppingest? Is this allowed? Shouldn't it be "most whop-ping"?

Answer: Yes, it's allowed. This is one of the few cases in English grammar where a writer has a choice among two equally established forms. This doesn't apply to all adjectives, but there are some like *brutal, civil, timid, wonderful, honest, winning, cheerful, cunning, crooked, loving, dogged, drunken, candid* or *damnable,* where the form with -*est* can be used for emphasis. What's more, the principle applies to other words too—whenever a writer feels the urge to add a little extra em-phasis. George Will's *whoppingest* gets more attention from the reader than if he'd written "most whopping."

Here is an opportunity to practice your writing skill. See if you can sneak in one of those unusual -*est* words from time to time. Follow the example of Mark Twain, who once wrote, "the confoundedest, brazenest, ingeniousest piece of fraud."

Little tricks like that can do wonders for even the boringest subjects.

wimp. On November 4, 1982, a *New York Times* edi-torial noted that the word *wimp* had been the fashionable term of insult for a political opponent during the recent election. "A wimp," the *Times* explained, "is a weak, ineffectual person, the 97-pound weakling on the beach."

The *Times* then listed five races in which a contestant had been described as a wimp. It noted, with evident satisfaction, that four of those races had been won by those wimps, and one was still undecided two days later.

Dictionaries are uncertain about the origin of the word. It was first spotted in 1959, but came into its own during the 1982 election.

Wimp may have something to do with Wimpy, a fat character in the long-defunct "Popeye" comic strip, who was always sleepily eating hamburgers. On the other hand, that theory may be wrong, since it simply doesn't explain the current meaning. But then, popular language is notoriously whimsical.

Wimp is normally used as a term of insult, and implies preference for tough guys. Well, as the election results show, lots of people think otherwise.

wino.   The Paris correspondent of the *New York Times* reported (1/22/83) on the appearance of Salvation Army soup trucks on the streets of Paris. "There were 16 men at the curb when the truck pulled in," he wrote. "There were a couple of winos, overcoats shellacked in filth." The rest were drug addicts, students and unemployed men.

Obviously the *Times* reporter used *winos* as a simple synonym for *bum.* He was wrong—winos are a step lower on the social scale. A 1931 magazine article explained: "The American hobo term wino is one of contempt and is used of those broken-down dipsomaniac ex-hoboes or ex-workers who used to drink themselves silly by buying ten-cent tins of sour cheap wine in the 'wine-dumps' of California."

So a wino is someone who is looked down on by a bum or hobo. Or at least he was fifty years ago.

The latest dictionaries are not interested in distinctions among poor vagrants. The *Oxford American Dictionary* (1980) defines a *wino* as "an alcoholic, esp. one who is reduced to drinking cheap wine." The *American Heritage Dictionary* (1982) says, "One who is habitually drunk on wine." The *New York Times Everyday Dictionary* (1982) says, "A wine-drinking alcoholic."

There's no compassion to be found in dictionaries.

woozy. Nobody quite knows where the word *woozy* comes from, but the *Random House Dictionary* guesses it's short for *boozy-woozy,* a rhyming compound based on *boozy.*

If so, *woozy* would simply mean drunk, and that's how it's being used by Pauline Kael in *The New Yorker* (10/4/82). Writing about a character played by Peter O'Toole in a recent movie, she says, "Drunk, Alan Swann isn't merely swozzled— he's liquefied. But in his woozy eyes you can still see his imagination at play."

But *woozy* has to be used with caution. It has proved so handy and descriptive that it's now used for any kind of dizziness, whether caused by alcohol or a knock on the head. The dictionaries now define *woozy* as stupidly confused, muddled, mentally befogged, dazed, psychologically uncomfortable, physically out of sorts, as with dizziness, faintness or slight nausea. If there's a definition that simply says "drunk," it's usually given at the end.

In other words, if someone feels *woozy,* he or she should be given the benefit of the doubt. The reason may not be alcohol. In 1909 O. Henry wrote, "A woman gets woozy on clothes."

workaholic. The *New York Times* (10/29/82) carried an interview with Dr. Kenneth Geddes Wilson, who'd just won the 1982 Nobel Prize in physics.

Dr. Wilson described himself as "a workaholic who takes a lot of breaks—a *lot* of breaks, such as folk dancing, hiking and playing the oboe."

The word *workaholic* can't be found in most of the major desk dictionaries. I tracked it down in the *Barnhart Dictionary of New English Since 1963.* It was coined by a pastoral counselor, Wayne Oates, who in 1971 wrote a book *Confessions of a Workaholic.* The book defined a workaholic as a person who "eats, drinks and sleeps his job . . . and drops out of the human community." Workaholism, he wrote, "interferes with their health, personal happiness, social functioning and interpersonal relationships."

Obviously, Dr. Wilson suffered from no such ill effects. Within ten years, Oates's dread disease had become a smilingly acknowledged foible.

wow! A few pages ago I wrote about the word *whee!,* used in *Newsweek* after a particularly outrageous statement by a government official.

To drive the point home, I'll quote the use of the exclamation *wow!* in the *Nation* after an equally outrageous statement in a recent book.

In his book *Wealth and Poverty* George Gilder had written, "Current welfare programs substantially reduce work. The poor choose leisure not because of moral weakness, but because they are paid to do so."

Philip Green, after quoting this statement in the *Nation* (2/26/83), adds the single word "Wow!"

Again we have a situation where a pronouncement is so

outrageous that only an exclamation—literally an outcry—will do justice to it. I don't know how you feel about such things, but when someone tells you that the poor don't like to work and that welfare just encourages their laziness—what do you say? Philip Green in the *Nation* said "Wow!" Gene Lyons of *Newsweek* probably would have said, "Whee!" You yourself might say "God Almighty!" or "Oh my God!" or "Gosh!" or "Jesus!" or "Cripes!" or "For crying out loud!"

But don't just say nothing. To be silent in the face of outrage is inhuman. When something makes your blood boil, for heaven's sake react.

yank. *Yank* means a sudden, vigorous pull. It's a colloquialism that goes back to the middle of the 19th century. It's such a picturesque, powerful word that it has recently become a favorite metaphor in politics and economics.

In a learned article about the Constitution in the *New Republic* (6/23/82) the author wrote, "FDR yanked Japanese-Americans out of the racist California of 1941." And in an article on "The Great Stagnation," the economist Lester C. Thurow wrote in the *New York Times Magazine* (10/17/82): "The economy . . . sometimes gets stuck in downward spirals in which spontaneous combustion cannot occur. The solution is a kind of Keynesian yank, whereby government pulls hard on the starter cord of the economy's engines by stimulating demand for goods and services."

"A Keynesian yank"! I've rarely seen the economic theory of the late John Maynard Keynes so clearly and vigorously described. You can see in your mind's eye the great national economic engine, the starter cord, and the mighty yank. The combination of the learned word *Keynesian* and the down-to-earth New England-type *yank* is perfect.

I wish economists and lawyers would use more words like *yank*.

yucky. Writing about the movie *E.T.,* the columnist George Will (*Newsweek,* 7/19/82) said, "The yuckiness of adults is an axiom of children's cinema. And truth be told, adults are, more often than not, yucky."

Yucky can't be found in most ordinary dictionaries. It's very recent slang and I had to track it down in the *Second Barnhart Dictionary of New English* (1980). There the word is defined as disgusting, repugnant, repulsive. It is a variant spelling of the word *yecchy* (with two *c*'s and an *h*). *Yecchy,* in turn, is an adjective formed from *yecch,* which tries to imitate the sound of retching. (English has no approved spelling for the sound of German *ach* or Scottish *loch,* so for a few years people tried *cch.* Then they gave it up and *yecchy* became *yucky.* Whether any reader responds with the retching sound is doubtful.)

Anyway, *yucky* means utterly disgusting, the kind of thing that makes you throw up. One example cited in the *Second Barnhart Dictionary* says, "Too many people say 'yuck' to liver because they have never tasted it."

I suppose you may hesitate to use *yucky*—not to speak of *yecch*—in your writing. But why not? The English language doesn't have too many words that are self-explanatory from the way they sound. Nobody reading *yucky* (even with its misleading new spelling) can doubt what it means.

Use the resources of your language as much as you can.

yummy. A movie review in *The New Yorker* (11/1/82) says, "The lilting soprano voice in the sound track song is yummy icing on Juan's yummy life."

Yummy, in contrast to *yucky,* is in all the dictionaries. It comes from *yum-yum,* which imitates the sound of smacking the lips. Naturally, it means delicious, delectable, tasting wonderful. *Webster's New World Dictionary* adds: "also used, chiefly by women, as a generalized term of approval." The *Dictionary of American Slang* says *yummy* in the sense of "good, satisfactory, pleasing, attractive" is used mainly by schoolgirls.

I gave this sex distinction some thought. I'm a man, and I would certainly not hesitate to say that chocolate fudge, for instance, or cheesecake, is yummy. Would I also use the word *yummy* for a sweet soprano voice, as Pauline Kael did in *The New Yorker?* I'm not sure.

But you don't have to follow my example. If you're male, don't hesitate to use *yummy* for anything delightful, if you're so inclined. And if you're female, and this book has inspired you to use the modern informal style, you won't hesitate anyway.

zap.   Writing about the competition among video game manufacturers, *Newsweek* (12/20/82) said, "Last week Atari zapped Coleco with a $350 million patent infringement suit."

What does *zap* mean? According to the dictionaries, it's an echoic blend of *zip* and *slap,* popularized in comic strip use. It means to move, strike, stun, smash, kill, defeat, attack, destroy, damage, overwhelm, overcome, strafe, bombard.

Zap, like every other slang word, got less lethal and less physical the more it was used. By 1975, when the supplement to Wentworth and Flexner's *Dictionary of American Slang* was published, there were four definitions listed: "1. To shoot someone. . . . 2. To defeat decisively. . . . 3. To confront esp. verbally. 4. To impress deeply." From killing to talking within about ten years.

Today, *zap* is immensely popular. Not only does it appear quite often in such places as the *New York Times* or *Newsweek*, but it's a special favorite of the popular press. *The Village Voice* (1/4/83) carried a top headline

Wap Zaps Willis, Willis Whacks Back (p. 10)

I turned to page 10. It contained a rather mild exchange of letters about a book review.

zilch.   The dictionaries are stumped by the question of where *zilch* comes from. *Webster's New World* says, "nonsense syllable orig. used in the 1930s as name of a character in the magazine *Ballyhoo*." *Random House* says, "Orig. uncertain; perh. humorous alter. of *zero*." *Webster's Collegiate* also says it's an alteration of *zero*. *American Heritage* simply says, "Orig. unknown."

This simply won't do. Why would a character in a magazine dating back to the 1930s give his name to a word first appearing in the 1970s? Why would *zero* change its name to *zilch*? And what makes the word *zilch* humorous?

My opinion is that *zilch* was coined because it filled a need. *Zero* means nothing and, in fact, *sounds* like nothing. You need a special word if you want to express the meaning of *absolutely nothing. Zilch* is not especially humorous, but it is most certainly emphatic. It doesn't just mean zero, it means "nothing at all." The *Barnhart Dictionary of New English Since 1963* has a quote from Jim Bouton in the *New York Times* (10/10/70): "Finishing second in the division or losing the league playoff is worth virtually zilch."

My own specimen also comes from the *New York Times* (11/7/82). After the elections in El Salvador a reporter asked an American official what leverage the United States had over

Mr. d'Aubuisson, the new leader. The answer was simple: "Zilch."

Don't shy away from this highly useful word.

zillion. Writing about income taxes, Russell Baker in his *New York Times* column (1/15/83) mentioned "zillions of exceptions written into the law to help the moneyed classes escape the big bite."

How much is a zillion? I checked the dictionaries and found that definitions range all the way from "a very large number" (*New York Times Everyday Dictionary*) to "an exceedingly large indeterminate number; a larger number than can be imagined" (Wentworth and Flexner's *Dictionary of American Slang*).

Zillion was invented around 1950. Why? Because people felt the words that meant large numbers just weren't large enough for this day and age. We speak of millions, of course, And we get more and more used to billions and trillions. We also have the word *quadrillion*—that's the figure 1 followed by fifteen zeros. We have *quintillion*—the figure 1 followed by eighteen zeros. We have *sextillion*—the figure 1 followed by twenty-one zeros. We have *septillion*—the figure 1 followed by twenty-four zeros. We have *octillion*—the figure 1 followed by twenty-seven zeros. We have *nonillion*—the figure 1 followed by thirty zeros.

Not only that, we also have *myriad*. A myriad is "an indefinitely large number."

Did people like any of those words? They did not.

The word they use is *zillions*.

zinger. To make audiences laugh, jokes have to be carefully prepared and delivered. Some are good, some are not so good, and some are terrific.

In the 1940s the word for the terrific joke was *boffola.* That sounds now old-fashioned. Since about 1970 the word has been *zinger.* "Bette Midler turns even moderately amusing lines into zingers," wrote Pauline Kael in *The New Yorker* (11/15/82).

Zinger comes from *zing,* which is defined by the *American Heritage Dictionary* as "a brief high-pitched humming or buzzing sound, such as that made by a swiftly passing object or a taut vibrating string."

Note that the old word *boffola* was formed on the basis of *boff,* which meant a belly laugh. So a boffola could be spontaneous or even unconscious—a line that got a big laugh. No more. Now we have zingers—the results of a lot of work and meticulous planning.

We laugh at zingers, naturally. But we know we are *made* to laugh.

zip.   *Zip* is an informal word meaning, among other things, vim, vigor and energy.

Three perfectly adequate standard synonyms, you say. Why use *zip?* Does it add anything to the meaning?

Yes it does, at least in certain cases. The New Delhi correspondent of the *New York Times* (11/18/82) wrote about the preparation for the Asian Games. "This year," he wrote, "sports have infused November with even more zip than usual. . . .

"New Delhi . . . is in the grip of fever over the Games, with a two-year crash effort to prepare for them, building in a bustling crescendo.

"Schools have been recessed and Parliament has been adjourned as the excitement increases. . . .

"Workers hustle to put the finishing touches on impressive new stadiums. . . . New streets and bridges have been opened. . . . Women busily plant brilliant red bougainvillea in highway medians. Fountains have been activated. . . . It is like the World Series and the Rose Bowl combined."

Vim, vigor, energy are old worn-out words, much overused and not up to describe all those feverish activities.

Zip is a 20th-century word, first printed in 1900. It's the only word that fits here.